Organisation
Development

Organisation Development
A Bold Explorer's Guide

James Traeger
and
Rob Warwick

Photography by Steve Marshall

First published in 2018 by Libri Publishing

ISBN 978-1-911450-22-1

A CIP catalogue record for this book is available from The British Library

Design and cover by Carnegie Publishing

Cover Photo: © Steve Marshall, www.drstevemarshall.com, @drstevemarshall

Printed by TJ International

Libri Publishing
Brunel House
Volunteer Way
Faringdon
Oxfordshire
SN7 7YR

Tel: +44 (0)845 873 3837

www.libripublishing.co.uk

About the authors

James Traeger

James has had a varied career, working in TV, theatre, as a graphic designer, painting backdrops for rock bands and adverts, as well as managing an architectural photographic agency, before discovering facilitation and organisation development in the early '90s through the work of John Heron at the University of Surrey. Since then, he has worked with a huge range of organisations, in many sectors and countries. His doctoral thesis reflected on his pioneering research into masculinity in organisational life. He was also a senior consultant at Roffey Park before co-founding the people change business, Mayvin, in 2010. He also currently teaches on the Doctorate in Organisational Change at Ashridge. James is curious about the relationship between identity, personal narratives and what happens in the workplace, a curiosity rooted in his own story as a father and as a descendant of Jewish immigrants to the UK.

Rob Warwick

Rob was a microbiologist before realising that people were more interesting. After a few years at the laboratory bench he moved into consultancy, working with investment banks, civil aviation, the UK's Ministry of Defence, commercial property and manufacturing; all affirming his view that people are indeed very interesting. Keen to move from advising people to implementing change and seeing its impact, he worked for NHS Blood and Transplant, during which time they supported him through an MBA and doctorate. As Head of Strategic Change he facilitated and managed many projects and became fascinated by the link between healthcare policy and frontline impact. This formed the subject of his doctorate with Patricia Shaw and Ralph Stacey on organisational change and complexity. As Reader in Management and Organisational Learning at the University of Chichester, he has now become increasingly curious about people's narratives and the impact they have on wider organisational learning.

About the photographer

Steve Marshall

Steve began work as a freelance photographer in London's fashion and advertising industry before switching to a career as an RAF fighter pilot. In the close confines of the fast-jet cockpit, he learned to obsess over the 'picture': the image of events shared by military pilots that reflects their awareness of what is happening around them in fast moving, complex air engagements. He found that a keen, accurate and shared sense of 'picture' is fundamental to group decision making and exponentially increases collective effectiveness. His doctorate used photography to explore our sense of identity and creativity and, continuing the thread of image and picture, he now researches and consults/coaches on personal and business vision. He has worked with a range of international corporates and public-sector organisations, and is an Academic Director at Ashridge where he is responsible for the Executive Doctorate in Organisational Change.

Note on illustrations

We wanted to offer a book that provokes an engaging reaction; an emotional and intellectual response. We have applied this principle to the illustrations and photographs. They offer contradictions, multiple meanings and unsettlement.

It is also illustrative of how life emerges and flourishes, often unexpectedly, like moss growing from the cracks of a pavement – that is our hope.

List of figures

List of stories

A list of the stories that appear in Chapter 9.

Foreword by Linda Holbeche

ORGANISATION DEVELOPMENT (OD) is often cloaked in mystery – what it is, what difference it makes, how to account for it. Part of the problem is seeing OD as an object to be defined and contained. Since OD is inherently human work, it tends to operate in complex – and not always rational – contexts and its effects are not always easily explicable. OD consulting is a messy business; the range of applications of OD is potentially vast and the very wealth of OD theory and practice methodologies can induce confusion and doubt in the practitioner about how best to intervene to improve the health of the 'organisation' and its members. Moreover, many OD practitioners working in the field experience heavy workloads that limit time for reflection and inhibit their ability to develop their practice. The temptation is strong simply to go by the rule book and to treat OD interventions as just a set of tasks. Yet to do so risks undermining the intrinsic potential value of OD.

This ground-breaking book, *Organisation development: a bold explorer's guide* by authors Dr Rob Warwick and Dr James Traeger, is intended to help practitioners liberate their thinking and develop a more helpful frame for their OD work. As leading 'thinking practitioners' in the OD field, Rob and James argue that in a supposedly 'post-truth' age, in which knowledge becomes an intensely subjective and contested ground, it is more important than ever to try to build a solid understanding around OD practice based on critical thinking. They call for a fresh look at OD that moves away from seeing OD as an 'object' towards using our reflexive abilities to consider the processes and contexts that we are part of.

This new way of thinking and talking about OD requires the capacity to look behind and around what is taken for granted and to challenge many assumptions which may have passed their sell-by date in today's fast-changing context.

It's about developing an insight into what underpins our thinking and that of others around us. For instance, in the digital era, notions of 'organisation' are under review. For the authors, OD knowledge is less about tools and more about facts and concepts that are consistent ideas irrespective of context; intuition built up over many encounters and the political, as we engage with others: laden with issues of power. As they point out, "We take into account the facts of the situation and our intuition as we make the next step in a process that is not guaranteed. It is highly subjective." Consequently, given the fundamentally human nature of OD work, the authors debunk the conventional wisdom of evaluation that relies on positivist measures of success which are often meaningless and miss the real point.

The authors encourage the reader to question fundamental issues such as who OD work is for − is it the organisation itself or "the 'life-world' of genuine relationships that exists within the business"? The conventional contracting process for OD work envisages "the facilitator as an OD person who has used their whole self, and has risked themselves to do something, not just because the business may stand to benefit but because these things, these people, their minds and bodies and relationships matter." They go on to highlight the risk in so doing for the OD practitioner, questioning the wisdom of investing "the human capital of our connections and personhood and the relationships we have developed, for the sake of the organisational system. A question is raised, about how much we really want to do that."

The authors write as they practise OD − personally, and reflexively − as they outline their own development journeys and share their personal insights from past OD experiences. Rob and James also cast new light on today's familiar OD dilemmas by engaging the reader in considering these from an imaginative and futuristic perspective that vividly highlights some of the choices OD practitioners may have to make. The themes they cover will certainly ring bells with readers. However, they also hold dear to what remains consistent since OD began, and what makes OD distinct from other 'people' disciplines; that is the centrality of humanistic values, with practitioners who bring their entire selves to their work and by so doing becoming key instruments of change. This is the vital spark that makes the positive difference.

This thoroughly refreshing, stimulating and enjoyable book will help OD practitioners gain a strong sense of perspective with respect to the ever-changing nature of OD. It will also help readers take stock of their own contribution from a critical stance and develop new thinking and confidence as they rise to meet new challenges.

Dr Linda Holbeche, Visiting Professor of OD and HR, Cass Business School, Co-Director of The Holbeche Partnership

Acknowledgements

W RITING A BOOK ON OD involves people, lots of people – it would be odd otherwise. Some of them appear in the narratives whilst others have nudged and provoked our thinking. But it is more than that: it is also about friendship and support. This has been particularly important to us in our project which runs against the predominant tide: the view that organisational life is rational and if it is found wanting then more rationality is the answer. This is our opportunity to say thanks to a few, but in doing so we fully recognise that our gratitude goes far wider.

We would like to thank Linda Holbeche, Peter Burden, Alfons de Laat, Heikki Pentti, Steve Ellis and Martin Saville who read and commented on previous drafts. We would also like to thank the 'Mayvin Community' which was keen to come together and discuss our ideas. In October 2017, over fifty people discussed the role that science fiction might have within OD – who would have thought such a lively and rich conversation was possible? It is true, science fiction tells us more about the present than the future.

We would like to thank Dr Steve Marshall for the use of his photographs and David Goodman for his hand-drawn diagrams. Both have given life and edginess to how our book looks and feels in ways that our words alone were not able to. To Linda Warwick, thank you for reading and re-reading our manuscript highlighting mistakes and challenging us to be clearer. And to Paul Jervis, our commissioning editor, and the team at Libri Publishing including Celia Cozens and Matthew Skipper, thank you for the encouragement and space to write a book that we thought needed to be written.

Rob would particularly like to thank Douglas Board, Alison Donaldson and Kathy Jones for our regular writing 'get togethers'.

With all this support, it is with considerable confidence that we claim all surviving mistakes as our own.

And finally, thank you to our families at home and at work.

Contents

Photo: © Steve Marshall, www.drstevemarshall.com, @drstevemarshall

An overture

W E USE THE ABBREVIATION "OD" throughout this book. It is meant as a shorthand for "Organisation Development" or indeed "Organisational Development". It could also be taken to mean "Organisation Design and Development" (OD&D). This says something about who we see this book to be for: people who see themselves as change practitioners within organisations, with an approach that is perhaps less about formal change management programmes and more about acknowledging and working with the life of human relationships. Also, people who are curious about their practice particularly as to why things happen as they do against the backdrop of a neat rhetoric of organisational change.

Here we explain our motivation for writing this book and, in doing so, relate a little about ourselves. We see this as an antidote to a traditional approach that introduces the authors to the reader in grandiose terms that create a separation that becomes hard to bridge. Our intent is to stay connected and acknowledge that we share a world with you. We therefore aim to *show* you our worlds, as opposed to *telling*. By showing we are not claiming universal truth; instead we hope that our experience relates to yours in a way that we can build on – hence the importance of introducing ourselves.

From James

One of my favourite sayings is that "we are all people of colour". What does this mean? It means that everyone carries some story of great interest and richness, connecting them to the wider historical and social weave. My own story is that my family were Eastern Europeans, refugees from oppression and poverty, who travelled amongst millions of others across a continent, finding themselves washed up in one of the greatest cities in the world. Which is just a grand way of saying that I am a Londoner. But my view is that, in some way, each one of us has a narrative like this. This is important, not only because it is just really interesting, but also because remembering this bigger canvas on which all of our stories are painted is important for our work, especially in OD. It provides us with some personal expression and the possibility of some confidence and connection; that is connection to everyone else and all of their versions of this grand and complex narrative.

This narrative is the stuff of OD because it is what creates meaning. And from meaning flows the things that matter to OD people: energy, inspiration and engagement, relationship. These are the stuff of humanity – all that organisations need in order to make things happen. That is part of my hope for you in this book: that in reading it, you will develop some enthusiasm for your own story and for the story of so many diverse others, not as some hero story, but as it is really lived at ground level. The curiosity and inquiry that this can unleash is galvanising. And organisations in this day and age, full of uncertainty, insecurity and flux, certainly need galvanising.

The trouble is, I often meet people who say "I don't have any stories in me – I am just a boring person", in the same way that people often say "I can't sing or paint". This is a shame, not just because they probably could be taught to sing or paint. It is like learning to drive: If you have never really had lessons and put in the practice, how can you expect to do something that takes a certain craft, as if it is an 'innate' thing? The same goes for telling your story: it is a skill to learn that has a craft and can be put to use, to serve a wider purpose; so that we can tell together the story of stories. We will at some point in this book talk about the notion of instrumentality and the idea of 'self as instrument'. In brief, this is the ability to be the change that we hope to see in the world (to paraphrase Gandhi). Being clear about who you are, where you come from, what you value and how that has all come about, may seem like a self-centred act, but I would argue it is the opposite. It is utterly selfless, if you see it as the creation of a piece in a wider jigsaw puzzle. I use 'creation' deliberately. That is because this story, like the wider story of the organisation or that of our human life together on this planet, is a constant act of creation. There is no fixed state. As Heraclitus is supposed to have said: "We can never stand in the same river twice". That is as true of us as it is of the river, or the organisation, family or community of which we are part. This book is about starting to see ourselves and the world this way, taking in the wonder of that movie that plays in our mind's eye and understanding its implications for our work in OD.

It is potentially a beautiful movie. It has its ups and downs, of course, and like all good movies there is a dark side, but in the end it is a great adventure. We hope you enjoy this adventure with us.

From Rob

My interest in organisational development has been long in the making, motivated by the question: how might we make the world of work a 'better' place? It was a question made more vivid when I found it hard to understand what was going on at work, particularly in the earlier part of my career. The rationality that I was used to in my scientific training seemed lacking in the power games and politics that I was thrown into.

Of course, my opinion that something was irrational was often at odds with the opinions of those more closely involved in the action. And when it comes to organising, that is our fate – decisions with good intent are followed by: 'clear' objectives, misunderstandings, reinterpretations, progress, head scratching, rhetoric of success or failure, mutterings and gossip. And through this process of communication and miscommunication, somehow, we make progress. But it could be so much better – and by this I do not mean being more dogmatic and 'clear'.

Here is an example. It must have been about 15 years ago when the organisation I worked for went through a 'culture change'. I remember the time and day vividly: 13:00 at the National Motor Museum, near Coventry, UK. I should explain that at the time I was working for a part of the NHS that provided vital clinical services, but one that existed behind the scenes. The day in question was to launch the new ambitious organisation with 'missions' and 'values' to enable us to seize the moment. At 13:15, the keynote speaker was introduced: a senior vice president of customer experience from a prestigious American hotel chain. With his roving microphone, he came amongst us, 50-or-so senior managers. His actions, arm waving and voice lent more towards Tigger from Winnie the Pooh than the rather quiet, introverted group that we were. He then stopped and sombrely told us to reach underneath our chairs to find an envelope. We did as instructed and opened it. The envelope contained a plastic card with our new missions and values. The whole experience was rather odd and was the topic of conversation at tea, and for weeks and months after. (The exception being the IT department, which was just interested in this new roving microphone technology.) What was it about this that missed the point? Why did the organisers think it was a good idea? There were many choices available, so why fly this smart-suited, energetic American over who was everything that the people in the room were not?

Roll on 18 months or so and an odd phenomenon was happening. Senior managers and directors were walking around with a book (and this was something odd in itself). The book in question was John Kotter's *Leading Change* (Kotter, 1996), a book that at its core strips the complexity of change into eight steps. Apparently, one of the directors had read this book and become inspired by it which led to further conversations across and down the organisation. And further copies were bought and carried around. Rarely did it seem that a meeting went past without mention of a guiding coalition, short-term wins or anchoring our culture. In time, the bookshelf was added to with Jim Collins' *Good to Great* and Stephen Covey's *Seven Habits of Highly Effective People*.

What fascinates me is how these conversations occur and how we pick up on, make sense of and then try to do something with these new insights. I read these books and in doing so became increasingly of the view that hardly anyone else had. But despite this, something *was* happening. These two events amused and bemused me. Other organisational development work was going on as well, such as leadership development programmes, coaching, strategy work and so on. During this process, I noticed people becoming increasingly confident and able to achieve things that, up until a few years before, would not have seemed possible.

What was going on? There was nothing like a clear linear process here, it was mercurial. Something was happening that was changing the pattern of conversations. These were taken up and responded to in ways that rippled throughout the organisation enabling further change to happen. Success was noted by our stakeholders and there was a confident buzz in the organisation. As a postscript, in these successes seeds were sown of future problems, of competences being achieved and tightly held thus limiting our ability to notice and respond to different challenges.

This is why I find the art of organisational development so fascinating and these are the themes that I'm keen to explore in this book with James.

The slipperiness of OD

There are many excellent textbooks that go into the nuts and bolts of OD. For example, we would recommend the book *Organisation Development: A Practitioner's Guide for OD and HR* by our friends and colleagues, Mee-Yan Cheung-Judge and Linda Holbeche (Cheung-Judge and Holbeche, 2015); or indeed, *Productive Workplaces* by Marvin Weisbord (Weisbord, 2004). Our intention is based on an acknowledgement that you may have some understanding or experience of the approach these authors set out, and yet you are looking for something more. Something that gets under the skin of what this thing called OD might really be about, as we experience it at ground level, as well as where it might be going, in this tumultuous age. We hope that we take you a little bit further along the track that we ourselves hope to travel, towards a nuanced understanding of how we do change, recognising the mess and complexity of human life as something to be worked with, and even embraced.

Introduction

What this book is about and why

PEOPLE COME TOGETHER TO work on some endeavour. This might be to make money; to achieve something worthwhile for their community; to share an interest; to seek power and self-importance; or because they are lonely. But often it is a combination of these and other reasons, and here lies the nub of the book: these different factors can be competing, complementary, spoken about, hidden or not even noticed at all. So how do organisational development (OD) practitioners work in such a complex environment? And where are we, as OD practitioners, on this list of features? OD is thus not simply a matter of the logical application of reason: we need to bring our entire selves to what we do, as do those we interact with. We need a new way of thinking and talking about OD. Let us explore this with a fictitious example about the beginning of the OD process – understanding a problem and developing a way forward – and how we shape common meaning from everyday words that we misinterpret.

We are in a London office in a newly refurbished 1950s building overlooking a busy road, traffic noiselessly stopping and starting to the instructions of the traffic lights below. Two colleagues, Sam and Chris, from OD are meeting the client for the first time in a corner meeting room of the open-plan office. Polystyrene cups, hot water, instant coffee in little tubes have been provided but are left untouched. Carol, the Marketing Director and client for the work, explains that her digital marketing team has just been formed by the merger of two smaller ones and there are tensions. She tries to find some examples. People are coming to her with small problems; they do not seem to have the confidence to work these out for themselves. A pitch that both groups had been working on did not go down well and there were rumblings as to who was to blame. And then there was Jane, who had worked there for twenty years and is now off with long-term sickness and unlikely to come back. Carol has her own worries. Newly appointed to the role, she is not really sure what is expected of her, particularly in relation to the CEO's new strategy that, frankly, she finds confusing.

Sam is an experienced change manager. Over a number of years and several projects, she has developed a finely tuned intuition. When asked to sum up her role, she cannot quite put her finger on it but instead abbreviates it to "I just get people together and get them to realise how they might work differently". In her role, intuition helps her to reduce a vast array of possibilities down to a few that make sense in the context and she builds rapport and confidence with the client. She finds it difficult to recall the complex array of judgements that led to a particular course of conversation. Intuition enables a shorthand of thought, and how this thought is described to others. She neatly summarises her intuitive mapmaking into a diagram and a few lines on a piece of paper that will form the basis of a client proposal. It was Sam's questions that enabled Carol to describe what was on her mind: for example, she had not realised the effect that Jane's absence was having; nor that of her own misgivings about her leadership role and the strategy. Somehow Sam enabled her to see these and make some connections.

Chris is new to organisational change. Having had a job in operations, he has moved into change management. He is keen, but finds it hard to pin down what the job is about. The sure footedness he felt in his old job has been replaced with uncertainty. The suggestions from Sam and Carol seem very short and lacking in reassuring detail. The conversation is not giving him the detail he needs and he becomes anxious, but sitting across the table from the Marketing Director he does not let this show. He finds it hard to envisage what the next step might look like; it seems confusing. Whilst he can follow the conversation as it builds, he cannot envisage the coming twists and turns of the meeting. He is drawn to Sam's diagram as an explanation of the meeting and ascribes to it more certainty than it deserves. After all, it was just a way of understanding one of a number of possibilities – but nevertheless one that made sense at the time.

Carol leaves with a promise from Sam that she will email her a proposal the next day. In a conversation afterwards to review the meeting, Sam and Chris misinterpret each other. Sam becomes frustrated with Chris's many questions. The intuition that has served her well in 'reading' the meeting is now a source of frustration. Sensing Chris's struggle, and unaware of how her own expertise led to a shortcut through the various possibilities, she comes up with an abbreviated overview of what happened and returns again to the diagram sketched in the meeting. Chris comes away with a simplistic view. Sam is also drawn to the simplistic, but for different reasons: she finds her intuitive abilities hard to recognise. So we have a situation in which the same words are differently interpreted by two parties; their meanings can only become clearer by exploring the frustrations and misinterpretations each senses in the others. In this case, this is true both between the two people within the OD team and between the team and the client. In exploring such issues, progress is made.

As OD practitioners, we hope that we bring about some sort of positive change, perhaps to enable people to work together more effectively so they can pursue the interests that bind them together. But when we write a specification of those hopes, perhaps in a contract, what are we really getting involved in? And what are we asking others to get involved in (both the people we have met and those we will impact, some of whom we will never meet)? We really do not know. These are acts of faith, particularly because, as in the above example, meaning and the interpretation of meaning are contested and always in flux.

Here lies an issue. On the one hand, we have a responsibility to do the best we can for the project and for those that are affected by what we do, even if there are difficult times ahead. But on the other, we have no certainty as to what we are getting involved in, apart from some rather generalised hopes and expectations listed in any agreement. All parties are starting a journey into the unknown, even if the first few steps are clear enough and we have a destination we hope to arrive at.

But our rhetoric at this 'contracting stage' is often full of clarity, assurance and confidence. And why would that not be the case when we will be engaging in a relationship with a client and they may be anxious about their reputation being on the line? We as OD practitioners will be anxious of our reputations too and how this work might lead to further work. Being anxious is a natural feature of how we work together, as is the need to show confidence and clarity; this is not an argument against such ubiquitous features of who we are. Instead, we are keen to peel this back and consider carefully what we do as OD practitioners *and* how our actions are reacted to in the course of our work. By actions we not only mean what we physically do, but how we come to understand, make choices and involve others.

This book is not only an intellectual argument; it is also trying to connect at a human level. In this context, knowledge is not only an assemblage of insights intended to create a logical whole; it also relates to how we experience knowledge aesthetically as a whole before we try to 'deconstruct' it. Imagine you are looking at a Mark Rothko painting in London's Tate Modern: what makes that art?

In short, this book is about how we can improve our OD practice by recognising and paying attention to the full range of qualities that make us a person and by appreciating those qualities in others. It serves as an invitation for us to be more reflexive and thoughtful in our actions and thoughts.

Like many in OD, we owe a debt of gratitude to Kurt Lewin and his post-Second World War endeavour to make the world a better place. But of course, the world has changed and become more complex and uncertain; thus we look to those that have sought to apply ideas of complexity to the world of work. The two of us do not see a distinction between theory and ideas, between practice and academia; instead, both are indebted to each other in an ongoing iteration of people's engagement with each other and with learning. We are therefore drawn to action research, action learning and the idea that learning is contextual; but in accepting this, enough insight can be had that is of use to others facing similar, but never identical, challenges. The issue of process and dialectics is important, of how we rub along together, to create something new and hopefully better. You will notice other threads of intellectual and practical heritage but they all in some way or another associate themselves with these ideas.

Both of us have been influenced by the work of Patricia Shaw, particularly her book *Changing Conversations in Organizations: A Complexity Approach to Change* (Shaw, 2002). Indeed, Patricia was Rob's doctoral supervisor. Within the Coda of the book, she writes:

> I have been asking [in this book], "How do we participate in the way things change over time?" meaning "How at the very movement of our joint sensemaking experience, are we changing ourselves and our situation?" This means inquiring into the ongoing local situated communicative activity between experiencing bodies that gives rise to intentions, decisions and actions, tool-making and tool-using.
>
> (Shaw, 2002, p.171)

Here, we have sought to explore some of these questions in different ways, for example by focusing on craft and art, the ethics of what we do, different literature and fiction. But we stay true to the idea that the use of narratives, and the micro-interactions they illustrate, shines a bright and useful light on everyday organisational life. We do not seek to answer questions, but to move them on in ways that might be helpful.

The arc of this book

We begin with a short chapter, 'The essential fluidity of OD and organising'. This is the nearest we come to offering a definition of OD. We do this from the perspective of how we have come to understand our own experience, which at times is confusing and contested. Indeed, we argue that the unsettled nature of OD is what makes it what it is. Later we explain our wariness of the crisp certainties that might make us hesitant of exploring our practice and the impact we have on others.

Change is complex and involves many interacting dynamics, a topic that we explore in our second chapter, 'How does OD work happen'. We challenge assumptions that change can be plotted out and executed along a number of logical and neatly interconnecting steps. We are not saying that an abbreviated way of thinking along these lines is necessarily unhelpful, but it is unhelpful if we do not carefully consider what is happening under the surface. In addition to the flows of logical decision making that might present themselves in the rhetoric of change, the issues of power, persuasion and politics are ongoing. Those of us who work with organisations cannot absent ourselves from these processes (to seek to do so would be a political act in itself), but our actions have important implications. The gestures that we make are responded to by others, who are in turn reacted to. Outcomes are therefore not guaranteed: they emerge from the interactions between all of us, through which we hope some beneficial change happens.

Next comes 'Knowledge, knowing and learning'. You will have realised, we are trying to challenge some of the under-examined assumptions about people and organisations, about what we as OD practitioners do and how we know. It is therefore important to understand the implications for us as OD practitioners and the organisations we work with. Typically, we privilege a form of abstract knowledge that implies universal application irrespective of context. This is problematic. In this chapter, we as authors explore why this is the case and what the implications are. It allows us to pay attention both to more comfortable ways of knowing as well as issues of power, cunning and knack that we see in the competent practitioner. We do not present these as a negative (although they can be, and this is an ethical challenge we will address later) but rather as essential features of how we interact with people.

When people get together they can be amazingly creative, resourceful and adaptable, and we address this in the next chapter, 'Artful practice to inspire human systems'. As OD practitioners, it is important to consider the nature, or the art, of how people work together. On a small scale, consider a workshop you have facilitated at which a moment of 'magic' occurred when people saw a problem in a different way that enabled an opportunity to be seized. What was going on in that instant, what was happening beforehand to allow people to make that shift and how were they able to contextualise and make use of it? Writ large over the entire organisation, how do these patterns of understandings come together and how is further meaningful action taken?

The next chapter is 'Crafting an OD strategy'. As OD practitioners, we need to work into these dynamics and occasionally destabilise them to allow people to relate to each other differently and see their world in new ways. To mirror the artful organisation, we recognise OD as a craft. When a craftsperson uses one or two tools deftly, implements, mind and bodily action become a unified process. They do not recognise the external physical shortcuts that can be picked up, put down or packed into a bag. Here we discuss how we might go about developing craft through the tools we use and the skills we develop. We do so with humility through stories, some of which are successes and others that are painful.

In this book we have written of power, politics and how people rub along together in the process of organising. Power is in itself neither good nor bad but a ubiquitous feature of interactions amongst people, as we consciously or unconsciously impact on those we know and, by distant connections, those that we don't. In the chapter 'Politics and ethics of OD', we consider the choices that we make and the impact we have. On the one hand, ethics can be thought of as a task carried out beforehand, in the planning stage, perhaps even involving the submission of proposals to an ethics committee. But what is also important, and often not adequately considered, are those day-to-day micro-ethical dilemmas that face us. These require a practice of continual attention and asking: are we doing the right thing, in the right way, to the right end?

It would be quite reasonable to ask us what impact have we have had in OD. What becomes problematic is a simplistic numerical explanation, based on a set of positivist expectations. Organisations are messy and unpredictable and these are the topics we address in 'The impact of what we do'. What accounts can we provide that usefully help us understand what has been happening in a way that might influence what is to come? If organisations are about *artistry* and OD is a *craft* then the way that we account for what we have done needs to be similarly *framed*.

The paying attention to ourselves within our practice is vital and here we address our 'Reflexive practice and social ripples'. Routine can be its own siren call, drawing us into the comfort of not noticing, particularly when things are going well. But this is not necessarily in the best interests of our clients or ourselves. Here we address what it is to be reflexive and how we go about prompting this in ourselves and others. In this way of thinking, being reflexive is both an individual and social pursuit.

We end with the fictional stories of Jas Porter and Imogen Sharp, set thirty years in the future. We turn to science fiction because it helps us to say something about the present; we are unbound by context and convention and become free to imagine other possibilities. After all, without imagination what else do we have? What might other ways of organising be like, how might we relate to each other differently, what are the ethical consequences if we do not speak up? And so on. This is our playground, a way of working with our ideas in the future present.

Throughout we use narrative, both real and imagined; this is our method, allowing us to show rather than tell. By showing, we hope to build bridges between our experience and yours and in doing so recognise your experience and expertise. Our aim is that you share our worlds in useful ways. It also says something about our method of working as OD practitioners.

Working with difference

Can a person act effectively or even ethically in organisational change if they surround themselves with like-minded people? Possibly, but it is difficult. As we will explore, our lives are made more effective (possible, even) by the shortcuts and abbreviations of our intuition that our subconscious nudges us towards. But being drawn to answers in this way can result in the exclusion of others, leading to their disenfranchisement, and social and personal harm. We may not notice opportunities to engage with the world in new and better ways. Moreover, continuing to engage with the world as it has always been is not sustainable for the future. This is particularly true of diversity, but in discussing this issue, we come to a contradiction and difficulty: it risks becoming merely an item on a meeting agenda, the subject for a committee, a section in a report. These are important tools for organisations and can help to draw our attention to a subject, but they are insufficient to make difference a part of the everyday conversations of an organisation. How can we do this? We have woven difference into the warp and weft of the fabric of this book, and nearly every narrative has involved engaging with different people and trying to see and imagine the world differently. If we look at the themes of this book as we relate them to daily organisational life, these include:

- *New connections* – how we might engage with other people and situations that we might not otherwise think of, particularly those with little or no voice; and do so on their terms, in their surroundings so as to understand more vividly their cultural norms and reference points that might hide between the common words we use
- *Connections and bridges* – this is not just about listening; it is about enquiring and sharing so that the conversation ends with everyone seeing the world slightly differently
- *Courage* – being courageous and putting oneself in conversations and situations that might feel unsettling; in doing so, we experience and sense the world differently
- *To slow down* – all of this can be 'done' but not 'experienced', by which we mean that we have rushed and didn't notice; it is important to

change pace, allowing us to change the way we notice and make connections that we would not otherwise make

- *Exploring our own differences* – to appreciate and understand ourselves in the process of engaging with difference; to think of this as being about the differences of others is to miss the point; it risks creating a 'thing' of difference, leading to a subject–object divide like that between the scientist looking down the microscope and the thing s/he is looking at.

Our next step

In short, we are paying attention to the humanistic nature of OD, its interest in how we are all interacting with each other to create a better world of work. To do this, the scientific and rational approach only gets us so far; it requires other qualities too. These are qualities that come to affect what we mean by 'organisations', 'OD' and 'our practice'.

Photo: © Steve Marshall, www.drstevemarshall.com, @drstevemarshall

The essential fluidity of OD and organising

IN THIS CHAPTER, we consider the nature of organisations and OD from a different angle. Instead of giving discrete definitions that imply they are things or objects, we offer a way of thinking about them as patterns of shifting interactions in which we are immersed. Because these interactions are a part of our daily lives, they can be hard to notice in our own practice and difficult to talk about. But this is important as becoming increasingly reflexive creates the opportunity to develop our practice. We offer this to begin the process of challenging and understanding practice. In other words, it is an invitation to ask questions (a theme we will continue throughout the book). It is not a neatly packaged argument in itself.

The organisation, or to organise

The organisation, or to organise: one is a noun, the other a verb. In the OD community, we often talk about organisations as if they are an object or an item. And in some respects, they *are* physical things: the buildings in which they are based, the legal documents that describe them, the contracts for the people who work with them, and so on. But in doing so, we downplay the stream of relationships that we are a part of: how we influence others, as others influence us. For example, in saying "I work for the NHS in…" or explaining that, as an OD consultant, "I'm going into the NHS to work on…", we are using abbreviations that take complex processes and wrap them up as objects. Here, we are going to draw attention to the *processes of organising*. This means considering organisations as patterns of human behaviour dedicated to some form of *organising principle* along with an array of resources. And through these tensions and enablers, people muddle on as best they can. This does not mean that any organising principle has been agreed by everyone; rather, it forms a sense of orientation by which people take decisions and move along.

In some organisations, this is stronger and more overt than in others, depending on the power of those involved; and in this process, patterns of interaction emerge and become increasingly predictable. These routines that people adopt, often unthinkingly, become culture. When we in OD talk about resources, we mean those materials and enablers that might be used in advancement of those aims such as buildings, intellectual property, software, networks of individuals and, of course, people themselves.

So when people use nouns to describe organisations, structures and systems, attention is often not paid to the verbs of organising, becoming, interacting and engaging. This also extends to policies, strategies and other propositional themes. Often these are discussed in terms of concrete outcomes, with little attention being given to context and how events unfold over time. These propositional themes are declarations of some future intent but accept that meaning emerges from the interaction between individuals and the context that they face.

Assumptions of organisations

There are some assumptions that we as authors would like to probe and, in doing so, we hope to encourage the practice of noticing and testing assumptions. We do not offer a definitive list here but raise questions to challenge the assumptions of organising, for example:

- *Are organisations a good idea?* On the one hand, they form a set of cohesive relationships around which activity is coordinated. They create a sense of identity for individuals as they relate to their teams and wider network. On the other, what good ideas and people do they exclude?
- *Are teams a good idea?* On the one hand, a cohesive group of people is vital in working, say, in an operating theatre on a complex surgical procedure. On the other, to what extent are the characteristics of teamwork stressful for those who prefer to work by themselves? Is it a contradiction that many in OD are sole practitioners, or work in small associations, yet advise others on developing teams?
- *What will organisations be in the future?* In a hyper-connected world, what will organising look like and will the demarcations that denote the limitations of an organisation today exist in the same way?

As you will see, we too use the noun "organisation" but with some hesitancy, knowing that it is shorthand for the verb that describes the processes of organising. With the use of science fiction, we do not take the organisation for granted. New hyper-networked ways of organising may just be too fluid for the structures and rules of the traditional organisation.

The fluidity of OD

In this section, we will explore the essential fluidity of what we mean by OD that is mirrored by the organisation writ large, the idea of which we have briefly touched upon above. There are three connected themes:

- How the part becomes manifest in the whole, by which we mean how an OD intervention affects the wider organisation
- The pitfalls and benefits of talking of OD as a 'thing'
- Bringing these together, how we can think of OD as something that is a contested and a continuingly negotiated idea.

To explore this, we venture beyond OD and HR by introducing some philosophy, a subject that can help us to see the world and the assumptions we make in refreshing ways. Firstly, we hear from James:

> The first time I put two and two together about what OD was, I was walking down a corridor at Roffey Park, an internationally renowned leadership institute. It was the early noughties and a group of colleagues were discussing how to handle a particular challenge with a client. I do not remember the details but I think it was something to do with managing the relationship between a manager and his or her team, in the context of some complex change. Someone in the group said "We'd treat this as OD. This is a classic piece of OD for us." This struck me as interesting in a number of ways. Firstly, it was the first time I had ever heard the words 'organisational development' being used in this way. It seemed to have something specifically related to the place where it was being practised; in this case it was being defined as a piece of OD work by practitioners at Roffey Park. It was the "for us" that resonated, as if calling it OD and defining it that way was somehow relevant for this group of people. For me, OD had become definitionally tribal; in the dynamics of our interactions we were defining ourselves and our identity by comparing our group with others. Often, this creates a sense of a 'superior us' opposed to an 'inferior them'.

> We often say that it has a 'local, timely and specific' flavour. Secondly, I realised that OD was something I had (sort of) already been doing for about ten years before that amble down the corridor. I may have called it 'facilitation', 'team building' or 'coaching' – or even 'restructuring' or 'systemic practice' – but this OD thing was the bag I could now put all of these loosely connected tools in. They were all instruments to manage the people side of change. Finally, the X factor that brought these tools together, the fabric the bag is made of, is the holistic mindset. It was perfectly possible, I realised, to do a bit of team

building, or coaching, without any regard to the wider system, and our own place in relation to it, as well as our own value set or ethical position. But only by having some regard to these does team building become something approaching OD. So, the local timely nature, the practice that brings the tools of the people side of change together, the holistic mindset with a sense of the ethical and values-based systemic choices – these may not add up to a tightly defined artefact called 'OD', but we may have to live with that. You might have to do some work of your own to define it more tightly. And that is the final piece of the jigsaw. What makes OD OD is how you bring all of these components together in your context. There are, by necessity, as many definitions of OD out there as there are practitioners. You make your own Lego with these bricks.

To discuss this further, we consider the work of Henri Bortoft and his interpretation of the German polymath, Johann Wolfgang von Goethe. As a brief diversion, we explore Goethe and other forms of knowing beyond the scientific, with its assumptions of rationality and cause and effect, that we often accept without question, even when faced with the trickiest human-to-human dilemmas. But back to Bortoft: he developed Goethe's ideas of science and his view of 'wholeness' as a counter to the current scientific tendency of seeing things in isolated units that we then assume can be aggregated to produce a whole (Bortoft, 1998). His concern, as a scientist himself, was that this aggregation of activity or insight did not describe the complexity, the dynamic interaction and the subtly of the whole (or 'system'). Bortoft uses a vivid example of reading a book:

> We cannot know the whole in the way in which we know things because we cannot recognise the whole as a thing. If the whole were available to be recognised in the same way as we recognise the things that surround us, then the whole would be counted among those things as one of them. ... But the whole comes into presence *within** its parts, and we cannot encounter the whole in the same way as we encounter the parts. We should not think of the whole as if it were a thing.

(Bortoft, 1998, p.285)

Here Bortoft is suggesting that the whole is of a different nature to its parts. And we hear this in James' experience. When we run a training programme or facilitate a workshop, it has some impact and we can measure and record this using evaluation sheets handed out to participants. We might even benchmark and undertake some statistical analysis, but the actual impact that we have on the wider system defies knowing in the comforting scientific way because the

---

*   The author's own emphasis

entity of the organisation and its organising processes are of a different quality to any discrete activity. This is not to say that the workshop or training event has no impact – it does – but we cannot be concrete about what this impact is. We must be trusting to some extent and encourage the trust of others too. In James' metaphor of the bag, this trust is in the service of some greater organising benefit – that the system will be better off according to some hoped-for agenda – but this cannot be guaranteed. We will explore this in more depth in our chapter 'The impact of what we do'. As we see with Bortoft's example, words and paragraphs have impact but they do so in how they fall away and create in the reader's mind the story of the book that is created by the author's intent and the imagination of the reader. Coming back to OD: this is why it is so hard to pin down!

We also hear James' experience of the conversation that occurs when colleagues use OD as tribal shorthand, as occurs in many professions. But something else is happening too: OD has become a thing, it is now reified. In tribal shorthand, this makes sense otherwise our conversations would never get anywhere. The experts 'get this'. For example, in the 'Introduction', Sam in fact she does not think about it, it is automatic. A consequence of this is that she is unable to notice these assumptions and shortcuts, and thus doesn't ask questions such as: what are the wider implications and what am I missing? To Chris, the inexperienced OD consultant, this is no shortcut at all: this is OD. David Seamon, a scholar of Goethe, explains a concern that the polymath had:

> Goethe emphasised that perhaps the greatest danger in the transition from seeing to interpreting is the tendency of the mind to impose an intellectual structure that is not really present in the thing itself. "How difficult it is... to refrain from replacing the thing with its sign, to keep the object alive before us instead of killing it with the word". [One] must proceed carefully when making the transition from experience and seeing to judgement and interpretation, guarding against such dangers as "impatience, ... self-satisfaction, rigidity, narrow thoughts, presumptions..."

> (Seamon, 1998, p.3)

One of the themes that Goethe kept returning to was the hard work involved in paying attention to the shifting and developing nature of phenomena and how we take this for granted. He was inviting us to pay close attention to development and interaction, and to consider deeply any recurring patterns and what they might be. This takes time but we are rewarded with a deeper understanding of the interactions that we are part of. These routines might be helpful or unhelpful but we now have choice.

The final idea we introduce in this chapter is the contested nature of what we mean by OD. We argue that this should not be a source of frustration; on the contrary, it is the rub or friction that makes OD what it is. This is a friction that exists between us, OD practitioners, and our clients; it is not a definition that will settle. We turn to W.B. Gallie, a philosopher who also had an interest in the process of how things occur. This is a short excerpt from a paper he presented to the Aristotelian Society in 1956 that makes a succinct point using art as an example.

> 'This picture is painted in oils' may be contested on the ground that it is painted in tempera, with the natural assumption that the disputants agree as to the proper use of the terms involved. But 'This picture is a work of art' is liable to be contested because of an evident disagreement as to – and the consequent need for philosophical elucidation of – the proper general use of the term 'work of art'...
>
> (Gallie, 1956)

In the paper he argued that it was futile to define concepts such as 'this picture is art', democracy or social justice in any conclusive sense. However, there could be meaningful discussions of one's interpretations compared with those of others. In doing so, we are not seeking the predictive power of the scientific method, but instead a deeper understanding of how the concepts have been used and understood over time and in different contexts. A consequence of this is that we should go out of our way to explore our practice and discuss it with others. As James points out, issues of context, our own values and the client all come to define locally what we mean by OD. But in these conversations we have half an eye on the longer term and wider impact. We should therefore not seek to close the definition of what OD is; rather the opposite: we should seek opportunity to understand that *the contestedness is the activity itself.*

Challenging our practice and assumptions

In this chapter we have sought to highlight the habit of thinking of organisations and OD as objects. Although these short cuts of reification might quicken our thinking, they hamper our reflexive abilities to consider the processes and contexts that we are part of. This has knock-on effects for the conversations and the shared meaning that we create with others; it downplays the shifting, contextual and relational nature of human interaction.

Experience of OD, experience of this book

What is your experience of reading a book? By the end, have you ever felt browbeaten into accepting the author's point of view, but rather resentful of the journey you were forced to take? As a practitioner in organisation development, would that approach work with your client? As authors we suspect not, so we are keen to avoid this here. In short, this is a process of joint inquiry with you the reader, one that engages the full range of knowing – logical argument, emotion, artistry, an appreciation of knack and even cunning. We have been cautious of being overly didactic, accepting that whilst we can share our views, backed up with evidence, other approaches work as well. That said, following feedback there are occasions in this book where we are now more assertive, more so than might seem natural to us. In short, we have approached writing this book in a way consistent with our OD practice: that of being reflexive, listening to ourselves and others as we make sense of what we do and make progress.

You can therefore dip in and out, following your line of interest; each chapter or section can be read by itself. With this in mind, we see ourselves as guides pointing out areas of interest, their implications and possibilities, enabling you to develop the ideas further in relation to your own interest. So how we come to do this is important, particularly going beyond intellectual argument, in fact challenging the nature of how we know. In light of this we will be exploring:

- *Narratives*. We tell our stories and those of others, drawing attention to events in the lead up, during and after; and how they weave together. In doing so, we appreciate that nothing sits in isolation, being instead connected to a whole lot of other activities and how we come to understand.
- *Fiction*. To appreciate issues of context and the assumptions we and others bring to OD we use fiction set in the future as a way of reflecting on how organisations might be seen when people have a very different view of what organising might be like. To do this, we have created two characters set in 2048 along with several stories.
- *Ideas and theories*. It was Kurt Lewin, the father of much post-war organisational development, who said there is nothing as useful as a good theory. And we agree, but are mindful that theory needs to be grounded and explored in practice. We therefore engage with theory to understand what has happened on a more general scale and/or to explore possible implications. We do so timidly because all too often it seems that theory and frameworks can eclipse what goes on.
- *Conversations*. Understanding our practice is difficult: it can take time to reflect on our experience. Sometimes this is best achieved in dialogue. In speaking of our experience, listening to ourselves and observing the reactions of others, the possibility of making sense of what we have encountered emerges. We will therefore include some conversations as a way of exploring both the subjects and how we might make sense of those subjects.

- *Pictures.* We will use some photographs, not only of things natural to organisational development but also to make other tangential connections. We do this as a way of developing the discussion beyond that of a logical argument.

The book therefore has several textures akin to walking on a gravel path, a wooden boardwalk or freshly mown lawn. The experience will be different, allowing you (and us as writers) to experience and notice differently and to explore different concepts from other angles.

As authors, we would like to draw on the meta-theme that connects the way that we have gone about writing this book with the practice of organisational development. Firstly, there is a relationship between you as a reader and us as authors. We feel it is important to state explicitly that you are experienced in your field, a specific field that we may have little knowledge of. We are therefore engaged in an activity of joint inquiry and at a point in the future we may meet up and discuss this. There is a similarity here between how you might go about having a discussion with someone who might be commissioning you to carry out an OD project – you are both experts, but in different fields. There is also the issue of power. Relationships are rarely neutral; they are weighted and shifting. Therefore, attention to this relationship and developing an ability to understand it are important. We are pointing to organisational development as a process of emergence, understanding, reaction and reflection in which we are all present. In other words, there is no privileged, elevated position from which we can view what is going on as an entity separate from ourselves. Otto Neurath, the early-nineteenth-century member of the Vienna Circle, put it nicely when describing the social sciences:

> Imagine sailors who, far out at sea, transform the shape of their clumsy vessel... They make use of some drifting timber... to modify the skeleton and hull of their vessel. But they cannot put the ship in dock... to start from scratch. During their work they stay on the old structure and deal with heavy gales and thundering waves. A new ship grows out of the old one, step by step... [They] may already be thinking of a new structure, and they will not always agree with one another. The whole business will go on in a way we cannot anticipate today. That is our fate.

> (Neurath, 1944, p.47)

One of us (Rob) was recently speaking with a master's student who had just completed an OD project that formed part of her assignment. The reaction to the conversation was telling, as it captures this tension nicely. We were talking about the helpfulness of a couple of frameworks that shaped her thinking, but also how they constrained wider connections and possibilities. On the one hand, she pointed out that this was common sense, it was obvious, that frameworks did not represent reality. But in a few minutes, having explored some of the implications in relation to her project, she pointed out how difficult this was. So what was the nature of this difficulty? An exploration of this helps to provide an orientation to this book.

To illustrate this, a framework widely used in organisational change literature is John Kotter's Eight-stage Process of Creating Major Change. There are eight boxes stacked on top of each other with one-way arrows connecting them down the page (Kotter, 1996, p.21). Each box has a number of bullet points with the following headings: 'Establishing a Sense of Urgency'; 'Creating a Guiding Coalition'; 'Developing a Vision and Strategy'; 'Communicating the Change Vision'; 'Empowering Broad Based Action'; 'Generating Short Term Wins'; 'Consolidating Gains and Producing More Change'; and finally, 'Anchoring New Approaches in the Culture'. Kotter stresses that change is complicated and he offers his model with "some trepidation" (Kotter, 1996, p.20). That said, there is very little by way of humility thereafter.

Such models can severely diminish our ability to explore other available possibilities imaginatively and to reflexively explore assumptions and biases that we all have when it comes to making choices. Back to Rob's conversation with the student: we have this framework that makes thinking and talking about change easier. It offers a plausible explanation of what has happened and plausible expectations of what might come. It provides a common language. But as we saw with Chris and Sam, the common language can obscure differences of meaning and understanding that only become apparent in conversation.

In this book we are offering the opportunity to unravel assumptions, biases and intuitions and to make them available for discussion. An example of an assumption is that of an ideal: an ideal OD practitioner, an ideal organisation, an ideal assignment, an ideal methodology. Ideals are often implied in management books and papers. They are utopian concepts and thus, by definition, unattainable. This is particularly the case when the difficulties and contexts are not considered – in other words, when we are not shown the detail in examples that readers can imagine themselves being part of. Here emphasis is on the ideal state, rather than the journey and struggle in getting there. There are no ideals, just people muddling along and in most cases trying their best in whatever endeavour matters to them. They work with ideas, people and physical resources to achieve this and, just as when a craftsperson fashions a piece of wood into a sculpture, each is unique.

In the next chapter, we explore the nature of the organisation; why we think of it as a thing when we know that what makes it work is relationships; and how these change and develop.

Questions invited by this chapter

- How would you describe the fluid nature of the organisation that you work with?
- How might you rethink the team and organisation that you work with? Do we make the assumption that they are always a good idea?

We often make assumptions about organisations and teams – for example, that they are static (e.g. the word 'organisation' is a noun when our work is of doing, namely the word 'organising'). We also assume that teams and organisations are a good thing. Perhaps we should not take this for granted in every case. How else might we think and talk about what we do together in ways that enable us to challenge our thinking? Also, what is the whole and how else might we think about the nature of the whole that pays attention to the interactions and their impact? In any organisational change, we are part of that change: there is no isolated position that gives us a clear panoramic view of unfolding events. In short, we are affected as we effect change.

Photo: © Steve Marshall, www.drstevemarshall.com, @drstevemarshall

How does OD work happen?

The work of human relationships

LET US BEGIN WITH the way that OD work gets started, not just formally but informally as well. And let's consider the implications of the genuine human relationships that we put at stake as we do this work.

At one level, the way OD work comes about is easy. Consider a familiar tool, like the OD consultancy cycle (Cheung-Judge and Holbeche, 2015, p.59). This cycle, or something like it, is the bread and butter of most programmes teaching OD.

It is a sound model, as it gives the OD practitioner and client some clarity about what to expect. The challenge is that life happens behind and beyond the formal stages of the cycle. So let us look at how that goes on. The cycle suggests that the process of OD consultancy has a number of discrete stages. Figure 2.1 is a typical version of this consultancy model, based on the work of Cockman, Evans and Reynolds' *Client-centred Consulting* and Peter Block's *Flawless Consulting* (Block, 2011).

Figure 2.1: OD consulting model
Based on Cockman, Evans and Reynolds' Client-centred Consulting *and Peter Block's*
Flawless Consulting

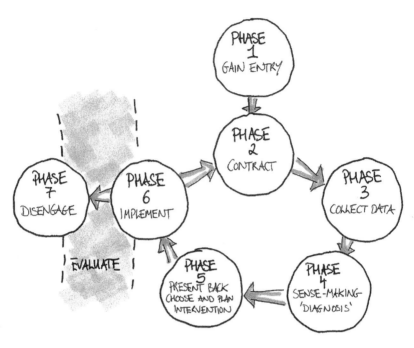

The cycle's stages are:

Phase 1 – Gain entry: the OD consultant is invited into, or finds a way to gain entry to, the organisational system.

Phase 2 – Contract: the explicit expectations of consultant and client, and the rules of engagement are agreed.

Phase 3 – Collect data: the consultant facilitates the gathering of relevant information in relation to the purpose of their work.

Phase 4 – Making sense/diagnosis: the consultant diagnoses the problem (either on their own or with the client).

Phase 5 – Present back, choose and plan intervention: some kind of plan of action is agreed and designed based on the diagnosis.

Phase 6 – Implementation: the consultant facilitates, or organises the facilitation of, activities or interventions designed to address the presenting problem. At this stage, there might well be some kind of evaluation of these interventions.

Phase 7 – Disengagement: the client is resourced to continue without further help or, sometimes, enlists the consultant on another cycle of activities.

This process seems quite straightforward. First of all, it suggests there is a clear need and that the job of the OD consultant is to come along and agree a way of meeting that need, 'gaining entry' to the organisational system. It makes OD work look straightforward, almost mechanical.

At one level, this is a good thing. It makes people feel clear and safe. It does the job of dealing with what most people are feeling most of the time when it comes to a new encounter – apprehension and a need to build trust. So in this light, it is probably a good idea to make things look neat and tidy.

The only challenge is that, usually, a real-world situation is far from simple and clear. Take the second phase of this cycle, which is about creating a 'contract'. A friend of ours has a neat saying: "sometimes the contract is a con-tract, as in a tract that cons us into thinking that everything is OK". What did he mean by this? We think to understand that, we need to look at an example of this cycle in action.

For this we are making up a hypothetical scenario, based on the type of work that often gets done in OD – think of the typical group meeting or workshop in the context, say, of some organisational learning. Let us say it is a leadership development programme, for a team that live in a virtual company, in a virtual world. Imagine this is an on-going programme, in a large corporation. It is one of a series of programmes for different tiers of the leadership population. Because the programme is experiential and lively, it is a popular feature of the learning calendar. We realise that this is a leadership development context rather than a strictly OD assignment, but we've chosen this because it is a context in which contracting occurs and OD work is often framed in big companies.

After outlining the objectives and perhaps hearing a little bit about 'who is in the room', the first thing a facilitator may do is give the group a chance to agree some ground rules. "These will form the basis of how we will work together. Let us call it a kind of contract between us", she might say. The group will make a list of things, like 'behave respectfully', 'keep things confidential' and 'good time keeping'. All is well and good. People start to feel less apprehensive and they can then get into the groove of the learning process.

Later on, say as a result of some learning activity, someone may feel like speaking out about what someone else has done, perhaps another participant. They may do so quite roughly, because they are under pressure, in the midst of an activity that is designed to be complex and hard to do, so it throws up all sorts of dynamics.

Let us freeze-frame for a moment in this story: imagine that these two people in our vignette know each other. They are senior managers in the same organisation and have come toe-to-toe before. They have, as you might say, some history. Although they have been professional about it in this leadership development event, the day-to-day context is messy. And the dynamics and history of this will come to affect what is happening in the room. Our 'contract' is not nearly strong enough to keep it out. The leadership exercise we have created is just a microcosm of the business's day-to-day life. It is here in the room. And although it looks like our two leaders are arguing over something abstract, they are actually arguing over something very real indeed.

This is, as Chuck Phillips (from NTL – National Training Laboratories) would call it, the possibility of the beginning of 'work proper'. If we were to pick up on this we might enable a discussion about disrespect, miscommunication, lack of confidentiality, bad time keeping and so on – in fact, the things that naturally happen in an organisation. It is only by breaking the contract that we can start to engage with work proper. We could start to untangle the conflicts and messiness of the business and bring them into dialogue.

That is where the work of real OD starts in this example – in fact we could say it starts when we depart from the OD cycle.

The same is true for any piece of OD work. It is in the transgression of the deal that work proper often emerges. So whilst the neat cycle allays apprehension for us and the client, it could be that it keeps in place the con-tract, the lie that things are OK and safe, so we don't get near the edge of dealing with what is really on our minds. It enables the client to open the door and for us to walk through to begin the work.

There is a deeper commissioning process however. Commissioning in this sense is less about the explicit contract; instead it is about the real human relationship and trust. It is about ourselves: our own instrumentality and the use of our own humanity as a tool. This raises troubling questions about what it is about us that enables us to do work in OD.

Let us go back to the scene with the two senior managers: imagine that the facilitator knows them of old as well. She has perhaps coached them or supported them informally in their work. Perhaps she is just friends with them. She has developed some real trust and traction in the relationships with both of them. So we go back to the scene in the leadership activity where she notices that they are blaming each other for the poor performance of the activity. She makes a judgement call. "I'd like to stop for a moment and ask you both what you think is going on." She says this with a lump in her throat. The room goes cold. The other ten or so participants in the room freeze. They too know about the conflict that has existed between these two managers. They have all seen it play out before. Treading with skill, the facilitator asks each of them to say what they think the other is doing and why. She uses all the nous of her relational skills, working in the here and now. She enables them to have a very real conversation about the interpretation of each other's behaviour.

This is a brave piece of facilitation work. But it didn't start with the contract they drew up on the flip chart at the beginning of the workshop: it started because they both decided to trust her to help them. Their pain was big enough to overcome their pride and they both were big enough to step into the circle. The work done was useful for them. It was also useful for everyone in the room and for the business but in a way, this was a by-product. For that moment of engagement, a set of real human relationships was at stake. What we witnessed was a breakdown of the stage set of the organisation and the workshop as a tableau within it. Through this crack, there appeared some deeper human contact and life.

Now this sort of thing happens relatively rarely and can be done in a less neat and tidy (and perhaps less dramatic) way, but we offer it to illustrate the point of what a deeper commission means in a broader sense than simply 'gaining entry and contracting'. In this scene, we envisage the facilitator as an OD person who has used their whole self, and has risked themselves to do something, not just because the business may stand to benefit but because these things, these people, their minds and bodies and relationships matter. Their "sweat cannot be excluded" as Bob Connell (2005, p.59) rather graphically puts it. They have put themselves in their embodied generosity on the line, because the OD work is a real thing. It is 'work proper' and is not confined to the walls of the conference centre or even the business. It is about humanity. And our choices here are about the permission we give each other to make real, human contact above and beyond the formal roles we find ourselves occupying.

This is troubling for a number of reasons. It asks us, for example, to invest (or if it all goes belly up, to cash in) the human capital of our connections and personhood and the relationships we have developed, for the sake of the organisational system. A question is raised about how much we really want to do that. To be sincere, like the facilitator in this example, are we not primarily interested in the 'life-world' of genuine relationships that exists within the business, rather than the business itself? Stephen Kemmis (building on the work of the German social theorist, Jurgen Habermas) warns us that this life-world is under threat when it becomes subsumed by the needs of the system:

> In short the economic and political–legal systems have become
> insensitive to the imperatives of mutual understanding on which
> solidarity and the legitimacy of social orders depend.

> (Kemmis, 2001, p.97)

We might even ask, do we collude with this colonisation (as Habermas called it) of the life-world, when we view these genuine relationships through the lens of what looks like a systemic tool, in the form of the OD consultancy cycle? We are not raising this to say that OD consultants should not use a tool like this cycle, merely to ask deeper questions about the values on which OD work is based. To get quality OD work done, we might want to consider what deeper human relationships mean to us, rather than assuming it is good work *per se*. We should do this because we are expected to put our own humanity on the line for it.

Life proliferates

The thing to note about this story is that, once real life breaks into the training room, what comes next is uncertain. Our facilitator chose to work without fully knowing what might happen next and against the possibility that something terrible would result. In fact, to hold fast to a particular outcome would be to risk breaking the trust on which her instrumentality is based. So she enters the unknown with only her intuition and experience to guide her. Although the strict sense of the cycle suggests we broadly know what territory we are in, and where we are likely trying to head, the deeper commission throws know-ability out the window. This does not mean to say she cannot have had some hopes or expectations. But this human-to-human commission opens up all sorts of possibilities. So, we are thrown into genuinely new territory together.

Going back to our consultancy cycle, we can recognise in it a certain degree of predictability, as if the world of the organisation is a kind of system that has a defined course. In this metaphor the organisation is like a machine (Morgan, 2006), a perhaps-complex set of plumbing or electrical circuitry. Its critical paths can be followed. Things can be researched, diagnosed, intervened in and outcomes then assimilated, and the system can be closed or reopened for another cycle. We are lulled into thinking that if we get the initial conditions established, the rest of the work will nicely follow on without trouble or deviation. We respect the yearning for this relatively simple cycle of unfolding but, at some level, there is an appreciation that when work proper begins and we are commissioned to step into the unknown, this metaphor becomes less helpful, even hubristic. So what are the qualities of this emergent work?

To address this, the story begins as life on this planet probably did: on the margins of a swampy beach. The tide is going out, and we notice that some crabs have not quite made it back into the water. The rocks nearby are studded with the remains of sea creatures that once lived in the sea. Like the crabs, they fed, lived and died as the sea retreated. Most of the crabs we find on the beach are now dead too. Picking one up, it looks like a beautiful children's toy, complex and intricate. Scoured of every remnant of flesh by the sea, it is like a craft without the pilot, the life force gone. We imagine it has simply returned into something else. It was, then it ceased to be. There was no pre-established plan to these events. There was no direction to the work of the 'blind watchmaker' as Darwinians call it (Dawkins, 1996). In this worldview, the role of the individual is to survive to create the possibilities of the next generation. Random variations may or may not be beneficial. It is essentially unknowable (subject to the laws of statistics and complexity) which of these variations may be advantageous. Like the facilitator who enters a conversation, they step into the next moment, not knowing if it might take hold. But we know something will. It always does.

As we experience it, at ground level, everything seems to come into being, to live and then to die, and re-join every other thing, seemingly without purposeful direction. From the perspective of the one big system, each part balances its own life, striving to differentiate, in order at some point to succumb to the whole again and reintegrate, so that the whole is maintained. Differentiating and integrating itself, it repeats. This is hard on the individual. Like the crab, we come into being only to get caught out, finding ourselves exposed on the beach as the tide goes out, and become food for the birds or bacteria that reclaim us into the whole again. We strive to live only to succumb, eventually and inevitably. Part of our makeup is to resist this cycle, eking out our existence as long as we can. That is important, because what we are doing is giving the whole a greater chance of perpetuity, by providing further conditions for random variations to take hold. It seems hopeless but it is successful.

To illustrate this, we turn to an article in the *New Scientist* that reports on a colony of ants found in a disused nuclear bunker in a former Soviet state.

> These ants... fall in because the metal cap over the pipe has rusted. It's a one-way journey... [they] are unable to reach the ventilation pipe to make it back home. Instead they gathered together and did what ants do, says Terry McGlynn, an entomologist at California State University in Dominguez Hills. "They built a nest and eked out an existence."
>
> (Malhotra, 2016)

Their efforts may seem pointless, without a Queen or a sustainable source of food or light, their colony is doomed. Yet somehow they have proliferated and maintained some kind of life. The researchers found upwards of two million ant corpses on the floor of the bunker, in a "strange, nest-like structure that the population of worker ants has instinctively built."

It seems like a sad story, this seemingly purposeless micro-world in the gloom. And yet there is something hugely inspiring about it too. In this concrete box, life did what it does: it proliferated. Random variations always have a chance of finding a way towards the light. These ants seem to know that and are willing to give it a go. Individuals remain doomed, yet the colony may stand a chance. This is such a strong impulse that we all find that this arch paradox drives our life. As individuals we strive to live as long as we can whilst knowing that we are eventually going to die, and all our striving does is somehow create opportunities for the whole to perpetuate.

Coming back to the organisational work, a substantial reframe is called for. The implications are manifold and we will now discuss these with examples from James.

Embrace unintended consequences

If life proliferates without an overarching design, what are we heading towards in our work? It does suggest that we cannot really predict how things will turn out. But we can have hopes and expectations; in fact it is vital that we do. Our own impulse to differentiate, to have some personal goals, like that of the crabs on the beach, is essential to provide the motive power for change of the wider life-system. So our OD work is therefore guided by our intent, paradoxically balanced with a curiosity about what might unfold, and an opportunistic spirit to work with whatever does, without expecting a direct link between what we do and what happens. In the words of business guru Tom Peters, "the unintended consequences of actions far outweigh the intended consequences" (Peters, 1991). This also means that we have to act as fearlessly as we can, without worrying too much that we will be sustained in the current system, because other places and roles for us will emerge. James draws on his experience:

> I was commissioned by a global company to work with the HR and OD team to review their workforce development programmes and come up with a better way of designing and running them. It emerged during our conversations that the HR Director of the UK business and their OD manager (and who had originally contracted me) were in major confrontation with the European Group HR Director. The dissatisfaction with the leadership programmes was only one symptom of a deeper malaise. I ended up helping the UK HR Director, through a process of informal coaching, to build their confidence as they decided to leave the business. The OD Manager followed. Meanwhile, through the 'data gathering' phase, I had made a good connection with the UK IT Director, who subsequently commissioned me to run a series of Open Space events, which were instrumental in helping the new IT system get launched on time and on budget.

Stay un-disappointed

The way we configure the OD cycle is dangerous because it feeds into our expectations that life should go a certain way. Yet as we have established, it is quite likely that work proper will emerge in the unexpected turns. It is also likely that what we set out to do, and what we agree with the client, may not happen, even if what does happen still brings value. That should not disappoint us because we cannot really know what we are there for until we start to stir the pot. Similarly, people often say "we've been here before", lamenting a "lack of progress". Yet organisations have a life with cycles of living and dying. This does not mean the good work we might be doing is negated by having to do similar things again later. It is like breathing. We are not disappointed when we exhale again. In this way, we should not be dogged by notions of progress. James explains:

> Years ago I was commissioned to do some development work with a small educational charity (of about 80 people in all). There were a number of different challenges that were raised in the commissioning process. The main tension was between the small group of about 15 teaching professionals who did the main heavy-lifting work and the top leadership. This seemingly intractable conflict went round and round. In the course of my data gathering, I uncovered a report, written about 20 years before by another consultant, also commissioned to sort out a seemingly identical fracas. The only difference was that this report had been written on a typewriter and mentioned the names of colleagues who had long since left the organisation. I held this up as an example of a repeating pattern that the organisation seemed to have. A discussion emerged that this should be seen not as a puzzle to be solved, but on the contrary as a defining and creative tension that drove the organisation to do good work. As one person said: "This fight is in our DNA". This re-frame eased the dynamic and gave people (so they said) almost a sense of pride. I suspect, if I went back now, that tension still exists, several years later, although I would hazard a guess that the story about it may have changed back again.

Focus on the small things that matter

"Small things that matter" is the title of a book of poems by an organisational development poet called William Ayot. It is a useful mantra for our work in OD because we can be hypnotised by the big plans whilst the best work we do is often in the moments of contact that we may even hardly remember. We should not dismiss the work individuals do as being inconsequential; indeed we should pay attention to these details. Our work is about building relationships, helping make a difference to individuals so that they thrive and grow. Sometimes organisations commission an OD practitioner because they cannot articulate the care and attention they would like to have towards their people. They temporarily outsource this. James reflects:

> I do not really have a problem with this, as long as I realise that the person in front of me, who they expect me to engage on their behalf, is a real person, and we can choose to engage for own our sake, because we are human. It is, again, about a genuine relationship in the moment. We need to have confidence in the knowledge that something useful will come of that, although we often cannot know what.

> A deputy director of a large team in the corporate centre of a university contacted me. They asked if I would help them and their team to step up to meet a substantial new strategic challenge. "I'll never forget what you said to me", he said, when we met up to discuss the work. We had worked together a few years before, during a leadership programme. "You said I had the potential if I took myself seriously. Well here I am." I responded graciously although in truth I didn't remember saying it, although I am sure I meant it at the time. I don't believe I would have said it otherwise. His team stepped up and now he is the director of that department.

The new broom will want to sweep

As with the point about staying un-disappointed, the natural cycle of organisational life means that when new leadership comes along, we may have to adapt quickly; and sometimes this is not easy given our tendency for hierarchical organising, as James explains:

> During the tendering process for leadership and coaching work in a pharmaceutical company, we suggested that we could convene an action-learning-based supervision group made up from the learning professionals of the different suppliers. This way we could benefit and learn from each other's practice. This would mean facing head on the competition issues between us, overcoming them and working collaboratively. This is what the company wanted from its managers who were attending the leadership programme that we were working on. It was a bold, creative and innovative piece of work, and it enabled us to calibrate our practice together and collect lots of data about the impact of the programme, which was considerable. They were about to commission the programme again when the senior leadership changed, a whole new wind blew through the organisation and the delicately formulated work we were doing was suddenly out of fashion. I remember going to a wash-up meeting with the new OD Director (who had taken over from our original commissioner) and when I explained to him what we were doing, he looked like a dog to whom I had shown a card trick. No matter how solid the data was about the effectiveness of this community of practice, he was not to be moved. We were not recommissioned. Such is life.

Notice when you stop being different enough

We also think that after a certain amount of time, it is inevitable that we become too close to the system and may therefore need to move on. Like the barnacles that attach themselves to the rock, once they become fossilised, they cease to be different enough to be distinguishable from it. OD work adds value because we bring to the system what it does not already have. Life needs variation in order to adapt. Our instrumentality comes from noticing important things that other people do not see or from being able to say things other people cannot mention. When you have stopped seeing things differently, or feel it is too risky to mention, it may be that your time has come. James explains:

> Once, I worked alongside a group of consultants who were engaged on an organisational re-design project. They had done a huge amount of detailed work analysing job roles, critical paths and work flow. They had been at this some months when I came along. It struck me that the whole of their project stood or fell on a substantial buy-in from the senior leadership team. I questioned them about this. "Oh yes we got buy-in from the board". "When was that?" I asked. "About six months ago", they replied. I knew that since then, a substantial number of the directors had changed. It emerged that they had not taken this into account and the project implementation was now at risk despite the fine-grained quality of the work. A image came into my mind from one of the *Pirates of the Caribbean* movies of the ghost-like sailors who have been on board ship for so long that they have started to form themselves into parts of it. I had a sense that these consultants had done the same. And in doing so, they had stopped seeing important things in their environment that they would not have missed when they first arrived.

Consider what it means to serve the system as a whole

We often find ourselves taking a step back and trying to take in what the system really needs. But of course, you cannot ask an organisation what it really needs; you can only ask the individuals who work within it. And different individuals will come up with different stories. There will never be one true answer. How do we stay curious, maintaining some integrity with the question: who or what am I really serving here? This may help us to come up with some kind of real-time assessment about where we should really put the emphasis. James continues:

> I was working with a top team from an agency organisation, on the borderline between private and public, looking to become more commercial. The team consisted of a mixture of people who were 'old guard' from the senior civil service and new people who had a more commercial background. They exemplified the tension in the rest of the

organisation between radical innovations and maintaining the integrity of a job this agency had been doing in one form or another over many years. The character of the chief executive exemplified this too: he was mercurial, likely to change his mind, which was a disruptive shadow to his dynamism. As a team of consultants, we debated whether we should serve the dynamic future or support the preservation of the quality past. There was no doubt change was coming and the organisation had to adapt but 'babies and bathwater' were words in constant use, and not just by us. There was no resolution to this as such. It occurred to us that our role was to live with this tension, like everyone else did, but find a way to keep the dialogue going.

Consensus is not the point – energy follows intention

The OD role is sometimes seen as touchy feely and facilitative, helping people get on and achieve some kind of participatory consensus. Sometimes that is what our role is about and sometimes it is about getting things to flow and move. Individual differentiation helps the system be clearer because it releases energy. Again I am reminded of the adage that OD is about giving the system what it doesn't already have. At times, I have found myself pushing where I sensed the energy was rather than just making sure everyone 'had their say'. Consensus and rules can be stultifying as James explains:

> A group of about 12 change practitioners in a large and complex system had the task of deciding what major strategic project they were going to work on together. A conversation ensued wherein a couple of people expressed some strong views about what they should do, and others voiced that they "didn't mind", as long as they came to a decision soon. At last the team had a breakthrough, when someone suggested that although they should look to find common ground, people could adapt what they did in their own context. "We don't all have to do the same thing," as one person put it, "why are we always trying to come to a consensus? It always ends up with a compromise". They agreed two rules for future consideration when trying to make a collective decision. Firstly, people had the freedom to adapt a collective project to their own business areas and make it work for themselves; and secondly, that "I don't mind" wasn't helpful. People should voice clear opinions one way or the other, as this helps everyone be clearer. As one person put it, "let's stop trying to be nice and go with what we have the energy for".

The questions this chapter invites

- How different is the pace and nature of change?
- How have relationships been challenged by the increased diversity of the more-than-human work environment?
- How has life proliferated over the last thirty years and what has its impact been on the world of work?
- How has this changed the way that we craft change?

What we have been exploring here is that OD follows some of the rules of life and evolution. When we consider how OD work happens, we find that it is about expressing our humanity and enabling life to proliferate. The mechanical model, which suggests a formula of easy-to-follow steps for how we do this, may seem attractive; and indeed, sometimes it helps to use a tool, like the OD Consultancy Cycle, to help people feel reassured and develop trust. But in the end, OD is a craft of life and it needs to be enacted with humanity. Sometimes this feels edgy. Perhaps humans, especially those acting as leaders, fear uncertainty more than anything. What may be clear from our future is that it is likely that we will face increasing levels of uncertainty, even with the greater reliance on technology. The mathematics of life will remain complex, literally and metaphorically. What makes life interesting is its inherent unpredictability. How can we learn better to live and work with this?

Photo: © Steve Marshall, www.drstevemarshall.com, @drstevemarshall

Knowledge, knowing and learning

Introduction

WHAT DOES IT MEAN to have OD knowledge? Is it about 'tools and techniques' or something more? In this chapter we explore how OD people 'know about' their practice. We maintain that knowledge is not a passive process of fact transmission between one person and another. We don't see organisations as machines that can be fixed using the right tools. Indeed, using a good OD tool with the wrong mindset often doesn't lend itself to quality OD, and perhaps sometimes a badly used technique but with a wholehearted intent can be effective. So what does this say about what it means to have OD 'knowledge'?

In a supposedly 'post-truth' age, wherein social networking combined with the degraded authority of 'experts' invites a free for all, in which knowledge becomes an intensely subjective and contested ground, we argue that it is more important than ever to try to build a solid understanding of thinking around our practice. For OD, this is based on critical thinking; that is, the capacity to look *behind and around* what is taken for granted. It is about developing an insight into what underpins our thinking and that of others around us. So our intention here is to lift up the lid of OD practice to see what drives it, in knowledge terms.

In our view, OD practice is emergent; it becomes vivid in relation to context and our interaction with others. We work to affect the context and knowledge of others. How we do this is in turn affected, tempered and sharpened by our histories, values and cultures; some of which we notice, but many we do not. It therefore takes work to build bridges of meaning and knowledge.

We hope to do that with you here. We think that knowledge in OD relates to the interwoven areas of:

- *Facts and concepts*: explicit ideas backed up by evidence often from objective sources that have traces of scientific methodology, these are consistent ideas irrespective of context.
- *Intuition built up over many encounters*: harder to define and implicit in our actions and attitudes. We act or make decisions without being able to put our finger on why. They are subjective and stitched together from a myriad of experiences. Difficult to give voice to and dependent upon context.
- *The political, as we engage with others*: laden with issues of power, in the micro sense we take a view on others as they do on us. We take into account the facts of the situation and our intuition as we make the next step in a process that is not guaranteed. It is highly subjective.

In this chapter, we pay attention to this broader idea of knowledge and take it forward in relation to how this book was written, and how it was intended to be read and its insights used. We include stories of participants sharing their own hard-won expertise of how members of learning communities grow from each other. And it is this we attend to here.

What might this mean as you read this chapter

When you pick up a book there are a number of assumptions that are made about what the reader and the author know. We may have assumptions about how the book will be read and you the reader may read it as if we have all the answers and you have none. This is a shame. We hope to involve you in a conversation that affects both of our worlds, so it is important to give voice to where we start from and the movement of thought to somewhere new. This reflects what OD is about – the practitioner enters the system as a co-participant in it rather than an all-knowing 'expert'.

Having said that, when you browse a bookshelf for something to buy on OD, you probably have the reasonable expectation that the author knows more about the subject than you do. Similarly, the author, emboldened by a book contract, can reflect in that glory too. The image comes to mind of a jug of water, filling empty glasses; of knowledge flowing from author to the reader. Perhaps this would be misleading, with the possible exception of the occasional person who picks up a copy who knows nothing about the subject. We take an OD-ish view, in sympathy with the intent in our practice: that you come to this book with experience and knowledge, like a client does to an OD practitioner. The point is that you have expertise in your areas and in addition to us as writers. We are therefore sharing knowledge on which we can all build and from which new understandings will emerge. Although the physical artefact of this book (or its e-equivalent) now rests in your hands as an object, for us as writers, our conversations and sense-making continue: the ideas never settle even if the words do.

So what are the implications? The ideas in this book are explicitly provisional; they are offered with the invitation that they may act as useful prompts that might come to affect your thought and practice. The relationship between you as reader and us is shown in Figure 3.1

Figure 3.1: The relationship between you as reader and us as authors

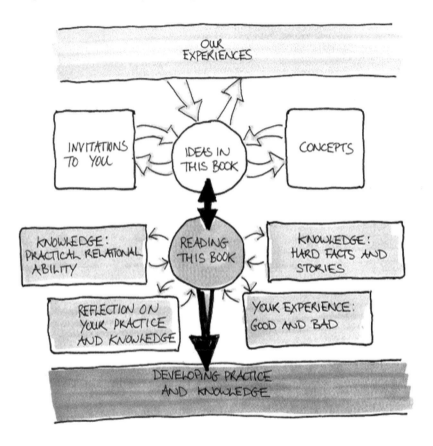

To explore the idea, we need to look carefully at how we know. There are facts: for example, that a snowflake has six points wherever and whenever it falls to earth. But knowledge is also relational: for example, over time we have the experience to know that we can explore a contentious issue with one group but would not do so with another. And when we work with that group we have developed abilities to work 'live' in a situation, of steering the conversation and of being steered by the group. This is a practical knowledge. Here we address the interaction of these forms of knowing; this is not linear, it is relational and contextual, as we see in Figure 3.1.

Nature and forms of knowing

Let us take the word 'tool', often used in OD to describe a technique used to engage people in a process of development; in this sense, a tool is abstract knowledge, a technique to be followed according to some predefined principles. The word itself is interesting. A tool, such as a chisel, is an object used to bring about some change in our physical world. A tool is an object that exists outside the person to be picked up and used and can be handed from one person to another. However, when we use the word in OD it can carry over connotations of its physical counterpart and in doing so something is lost. We can fail to engage fully with the fact that we are talking about how people come together, have conversations and go away probably with a differing view of the world. Instead of discussing ephemeral ideas and possibilities of how views and opinions will change, we reasonably abbreviate and talk of concepts of a 'world café', 'focus group', 'workshop', 'observations' and 'action learning' but do so as if they are concrete or discrete entities.

In the 'wrong hands', a tool can be used in a way that fails to pay attention to the subtle contexts, human dynamics and relationships that are present from one group of people to another, with histories often going back many years. The highly experienced OD practitioner will intuitively sense these things, ask questions and be curious about the goings on in the organisation; how people relate to each other, issues of power, who knows what and so forth. A tool in the hands of a person experienced in their craft becomes part of that person.

This has a number of implications. To illustrate, let us take the tool of action learning. Let's consider an experienced facilitator, explaining action learning to a group of say six people who are new to the process. The facilitator is likely to go through a number of steps, perhaps accompanied by some slides. At this point it seems abstract. At the start of action learning, the facilitator walks them through the process: stating the problem; working with the group to define it in more detail, encouraging open questions that enable the person to see their problem in a different light; and finally identifying a number of actions for them to take. It seems cumbersome at first, like trying on an ill-fitting suit. Roll forward a few months: conversations are had and actions are identified yet no-one is referring to the process; the people in the set have become expert in managing their relationships.

Perhaps the facilitator might add a few comments of challenge when the conversation is too comfortable or a nudge when it becomes stuck. In this sense, the tool has developed a different quality. Like a chisel in the hands of an expert woodworker that becomes almost a part of their body, it is no longer thought about when used. In a different instance, consider a facilitator who is new to this role. They might find it hard to negotiate clearly, offer too many expert models and ideas for fear of feeling like they don't 'add value', therefore crowding out the space for others in the group to engage. They may half realise they need to let go of being in charge but find it hard to do so. Overly concerned with doing it right, they may not relax enough to engender a relaxed mood in the space between them.

In this sense, we are all developing and are part of an interacting process with each other. Sometimes this is obvious and clear; at other times it is a process we do not notice. OD knowledge, in this case, is nuanced, emergent, timely and local; and the tool is *within* rather than *between* the people involved.

This captures the essence what we are interested in. It is less about precise use of techniques but more about how we understand the relationships that we become part of when we are involved in OD. It is a relationship that is essential to OD practice and extends to the reading of this book.

An example from Rob – the many ways of organ donation:

> We would like to illustrate this with an example, set in the world of healthcare in the UK. Imagine facilitating a workshop. It is a bright and sunny day, if not a little cold. We have booked a large room at a London university. It is a place of quietness in the heart of London just a few hundred metres from the rush of Madam Tussauds and Baker Street. The room is laid out with a number of round tables in 'cabaret style' each with a thick red cloth. On each table there is a piece of paper (size A0) with a diagram. This diagram has taken weeks to prepare and is the result of hundreds of miles of travel throughout the UK and many conversations, gathering 'data'. The subject is organ donation in the UK, namely the process of organ removal and how it be improved to ensure better outcomes for the patients who would receive them. There are about twenty surgical teams across the country. Prior to the meeting, we met with most of them and discussed what they did, sketching it out on a process map, a diagram showing who does what in relation to others.
>
> These conversations involved theatre nurses, surgeons, anaesthetists, specialist nurses in organ donation and so on. What struck us is how keen people were to talk with us, but more importantly how different their approaches are, although the language they used was almost identical. The question we pondered was: does this matter? Issues of patient safety, cost and efficiency are all vital factors. So we prepared the process maps, highlighting areas of 'consensus' and questions to

explore. In undertaking our 'UK tour' we were getting to know people, how their teams organised themselves, who had power (both formally, and who quietly made the cogs turn) and how organ retrieval fits in with all the other activities they have to do. But there was something else: many found describing their routine activities, built up in their teams over many years, very difficult. This was "just what we do..." they'd explain. We also heard about the emotional and physical toil. For example, one surgeon became upset when recounting the impact of working through the night knowing the busy nature of the day ahead.

On the one hand, we have these highly complex and contextual activities involving many people woven into different activities of the hospital and, on the other, a lack of words to describe this richness. But in those visits, walking around the wards, having conversations in tearooms, attending formal presentations and taking meals in staff restaurants, other pictures emerged that gave us a glimpse of the invisible context in which these people navigate so skilfully. By comparison we felt keenly like outsiders, but with intent to help, as best we can.

Back to the day at the university in London. People file in from around the UK and take their places at the tables – one for each team. Fire exits are pointed out, arrangements for lunch and breaks are explained before we go through the purpose of the day, something along the lines of "what is your process, what are the important steps and why?" In front of them are the large process maps developed from our conversations along with coloured marker pens and post-it notes. Over a period of time, the neatness of the printed sheets becomes obscured with coloured inks and little pieces of paper. The noise in the room is a constant chatter with one or two occasionally distracted by their phones. We then move around, sharing understanding of what the different teams did, explaining and re-explaining with words that become increasingly less taken for granted. Late afternoon and everyone leaves each with a different view of their practice, including us as facilitators, along with some consensus as to what the important steps are and what a new future might look like. This is not neatly or fully agreed; there is more work to do and people have arranged to have further conversations. On the surface, the output of the meeting is a new process map that is included in a governmental policy document, but under the surface new understandings and relationships are starting to develop along with new networks and the potential for different conversations.

Although the situation was unique, what happened was typical. So what are the points worth noting from this narrative? What kind of know-how does it suggest we exhibited as we went about our work here?

We could consider it in the light of the work of the South American Community Organiser, Paulo Freire. Freire, who was heavily influenced by Karl Marx, wrote a landmark book *Pedagogy of the Oppressed* in the late 1960s (Freire, 1996). He was keen to argue that education must lead to some positive social change; it is more than just filling people's heads with knowledge – it has to achieve something. In relation to the case above, education is about us in the context in which we found ourselves and the problems people face on a day-to-day basis. For Freire it is always unfinished, requiring dialogue between educators and those being educated (in fact he is sceptical of this distinction) and there are no fixed answers. To be effective we need to be aware of what is around us and to react to these changing situations. This combination of dealing with real-life practical issues, being more aware of how we are with people and this overriding drive for social good is vital.

In the above, do we position ourselves as educators? Perhaps not, but we are a convenor, a facilitator, someone who enables conversations to be had that would otherwise not occur, and a stimulant of self-reflection. There are similarities with Freire's approach. As a community, working in different organisations, spread over the UK there is a growing awareness of other people's practice, both similar and different. There are conversations as to what matters and what doesn't. Many of the people involved are of high status in their organisations and some are also representing their professional bodies; one can almost sense the consistencies and power relations standing behind them. That said, perhaps we helped to foster some good humour and a willingness to listen. Our role seems to come in and out of the picture. Ironically, where we may be most effective is when we are just observing people talking, hunched over the paper with pens in their hands – the conditions having been nurtured for those conversations to happen.

Freire was keen to stress the importance of modesty and the encouragement of critical thinking. In explaining that "dialogue cannot exist without humility" he points out poetically:

> How can I dialogue if I always project ignorance onto others and never perceive my own? How can I dialogue if I regard myself as a case apart from others – mere 'its' in whom I cannot recognise others 'I's? How can I dialogue if I consider myself a member of the in-group of 'pure' [people], the owners of truth and knowledge, for whom all non-members are 'these people'...? How can I dialogue if I'm afraid of being displaced...?
>
> (Freire, 1996, pp.71–2)

He further points out that this requires a realistic faith that people have the ability to understand and create something new. Freire prompts us as facilitators to a paradoxical position of assertive humility. We are assertive in the sense of enabling a process and to encourage people to have confidence with each other. Occasionally that means being quite bossy and authoritative, but with humility in the sense that, when things are working well, we melt into the background. By working in this way, knowledge is being created by different understandings being shared, new networks and connections being made and a critical awareness of what is important developed. On the issue of critical thinking, it is again worth considering Freire's words:

> True dialogue cannot exist unless the dialoguers engage in critical thinking – thinking which discerns an indivisible solidarity between the world and the people and admits of no dichotomy between them – thinking which perceives reality as process, as transformation, rather than as a static entity – thinking which does not separate itself from action...

> (Freire, 1996, p.73)

This requires some unpicking. To use a scientific metaphor, critical thinking in this context is not a microscope whereby the individual is separate from the phenomena. We are part of a transformative social process whereby we all change and develop. This includes us as facilitators. There is no separate reality that is to be discovered, like turning over a rock on the beach. But what does this say for us as facilitators? We are a part of the exploration and we were part of a political process, with complex power relations that take time to understand sufficiently. And as we act into this political process we create ripples in the power relations. These power relations only become evident when disturbed. This causes people to notice and prompts them to engage in conversations.

Another example – of where it goes wrong!

In the above narrative, the outcome is positive, but of course this isn't always the case; events can take a surprising and sometimes hurtful turn, but one that nevertheless provides learning as Rob explains:

> Let us consider another case involving a good friend and colleague and me. It involves the subject of trust and power. Let's say we have been asked to run a workshop about this subject for some HR professionals. We decide in the planning to do a 'fishbowl' exercise and take the risk of putting ourselves at the centre of it, as an illustration of our trust in each other and the group. A conversation progresses, with three of us on chairs in the middle of a circle, surrounded by the rest of the group. Their brief is to notice what themes of trust emerge in our conversations. This is to be discussed further in smaller groups before coming back in a plenary session. The themes that emerge include: how we got to know each other; how we misinterpret the expectations

of each other; how this leads to further discussions; issues of power as we work with each other; our vulnerabilities; and how we show these and how we respond to them.

Our initial reaction is that it went well. We have a break followed by the smaller conversations. And then it starts. From one quarter of the group, one of us is accused of not setting up the roles and responsibilities clearly, of how misusing power, of failing to be clear right at the beginning about how it was all to work. This carries on for about 10 minutes and as we look around, we are dumb struck. Could we have predicted this? Or is it the reaction of one or two individuals? Probably. Is it startling? Certainly. As we reflect on this afterwards we mull over a lack of keenness to explore the phenomena of trust and the leap to judgement. We notice we may have used certain language that sat at odds with the audience. The word 'power', for example, seems to have been like the proverbial red rag. People seem to think we are implying how powerful we are. These terms were taken up differently among some of the group and this came back to us in the form of accusation rather than exploration. We hadn't come across as humble – perhaps rather than appearing vulnerable and trusting, and inquiring about power, we inadvertently set ourselves up as powerful; as the centre of attention. We had misunderstood our worlds, leading to a visceral jarring of understanding.

Using these narratives we can explore two different concepts of knowledge and knowing. The first is *Epistêmê*, the sense of abstract knowledge highly valued in academic circles; the second is *Mêtis*, that of practical wisdom, cunning and knack associated with the world of practice. Let's consider the relationship between the two.

Mêtis was a Greek god and wife of Zeus known for her cunning and wisdom. The modern interpretation of *Mêtis* has been explored in a number of ways, including: as an everyday practice that goes unnoticed (DeCerteau, 1984), in relation to how people engage with public policy (Scott, 1998), in terms of other forms of knowledge (Baumard, 1999) and from the perspective of Homer's Iliad (Detienne and Vernant, 1991). These different tacks say something about the slippery nature of this form of knowledge, namely that it resists being pinned down; the nearest we get is Detienne and Vernant's explanation that it is:

a complex but very coherent body of mental attitudes and intellectual behaviour which combine flair, wisdom, forethought, subtlety of mind, deception, resourcefulness, vigilance, opportunism, various skills, and experience acquired over the years. It is applied to situations which are transient, shifting, disconcerting and ambiguous, situations which do not lend themselves to precise measurement, exact calculation, or rigorous logic.

(Detienne and Vernant, 1991, p.3)

People find inventive ways to interact, make sense and exploit, for good or ill, clear-cut instructions in the form of policy, regulation or some explained future state that seemed 'obvious' to those who drafted them. This might include a strategy for implementing some form of organisational improvement or an HR initiative aimed at increasing diversity or, as in the case above, attempting to get people from different organisations to work more closely together.

In the first example above, we worked to make the knowledge of others explicit (both to themselves and others) and to enable people to find the words to articulate their practice. The people that had gathered for this workshop were all expert in the politics and power play of their institutions and adept at 'getting things done' but this wasn't a voiced expertise: often, it had been built up tacitly over many years through their networks and 'working out what works'. The issue faced was how people were to make sense of and interpret some broad policy statements issued by a government department. This was in relation to increased investment but also how they were to work with teams in other organisations to provide a more connected service. There was no set formula and what was understood as being 'good' was not clear. In fact, clarity had been omitted at the policy stage in order to ensure agreement, an act of *Mêtis* in a policy community.

This form of conjectural knowledge is highly mutable and ephemeral, even furtive. There is a practical nature about it where events play out over time. Here actions are akin to a dance, where the partners know each other in an almost unnoticeable process, only made evident when mistakes occur or new people arrive. Here the goal is not clear but it continually shifts and develops as new opportunities or challenges are sensed in the moment. It is therefore highly emergent and somewhat hidden. This was the context being played out in the first narrative and brought to a head in a piece of crafted choreography for the workshop. In convening the workshop we were using these skills – encouraging people to make sense and interpret the policy, but doing so in a way that is true to the intent of the policy makers. But of course, this doesn't always work. We can all exhibit our skills, our *Mêtis* (or lack thereof) somewhat clumsily on occasions. The second example clearly shows what happens when we misunderstand the world we are working in.

Let's contrast this with *Epistêmê*. This is the type of knowledge that aligns itself with the scientific method. Here ideas are generated, hypotheses tested and evidence sought with the aim of producing knowledge that will be true irrespective of context. But of course, in working with people, contexts change and how we interact with each other shifts, as the two narratives above show. The assumption with *Epistêmê* is that knowledge requires the objective perspective from which a number of variables can be adjusted so as to test and prove our previously defined thinking. It is thus a sequential form of knowledge where we plan our route to understanding.

The outcome of this is clearly defined principles, the implication being that, from a firm start, events should run like clockwork. This heavy scientific footprint can be found in the field of OD, as it can in strategy, planning and the neoliberal agenda more generally. To give an example, several years ago the NHS Institute for Innovation and Improvement produced a spiral-bound guide to large-scale change (Bevan, 2011; Bevan et al., 2011). We choose this example not because it is unusual but rather the opposite. In it we see a number of tools such as 'polarity mapping', 'mindset shifting', 'the discovery model', 'world café' and so forth. We also have an emerging model of large-scale change with seven boxes with arrows going in circles and straight lines. Here we see all of the representative features of epistemic knowledge with very little attention given to political and power relations, how we make sense of the present that we are experiencing and the cunning and knack that guides us.

What we are keen to do is explore the interaction between *Mêtis* and *Epistêmê* explicitly located within a shifting field of context, two examples of which are included in the narratives above. They exist in a paradoxical relationship with each other, where each is reliant on the other. However, there is a tension; a collapse in one leads to the relationship faltering. This form of paradoxical relationship is explained by the complexity writer Ralph Stacey:

> Paradox [is] a state in which two diametrically opposing forces/ideas are simultaneously present, neither of which can ever be resolved or eliminated. There is, therefore, no possibility of a choice between the opposing poles or of locating them in different spheres. Instead, what is required is a different kind of logic, such as the dialectical logic of Hegel. In this kind of logic, the word 'paradox' means presence together at the same time of contradictory, essentially conflicting ideas, none of which can be eliminated or resolved. Indeed it is this conflict that gives rise to transformation that is central to Hegel's dialectical logic. ... Essential to Hegel's dialectical logic is its social dimension.

(Stacey, 2006, pp.241–2)

These interactions are hard to notice and harder still to write down; they exist fleetingly. Take the second narrative, for example: on the one hand, deep emotional anxiety along with a strong physiological response; but on the other, we may also feel sufficiently detached to be able to be fascinated by what was going on. We can still notice the vivid detail of how people are interacting with each other and the expression on their faces; even notice acutely how we are reacting, in what Petrushka Clarkson called "midsight", that is the ability to notice even when we are in the midst of something compelling (Clarkson, 1993). And in this process of being detached and involved (Warwick, 2016) we may form a way forward and an ability to interact meaningfully that is worthwhile, respectful and safe enough – although not too safe that learning can't take place. The point is that we can't do that work beforehand, other than to consider a few possibilities; it is emergent and relational.

In the first narrative we hear the different forms of knowledge at play with each person mindful of the constituencies of which they are part. We are always pursuing an agenda, compromising, shifting, taking advantage as we go along and being mindful of how we are perceived. These are all characteristics of *Mêtis*. Epistemic knowledge provided vital substance on which concrete conversations could be had. In fact, in the second narrative we see where this relationship breaks down. Our language is fateful. Let's consider the use of a word like 'power'. We may mean it in a very specific and academic sense, with reference to that power which is a factor in all human relationships. We may not mean it as a way of getting our way over another person, but that is how it may be taken by others. There is room for a misunderstanding, which can lead to a sudden fracture of the group. If we had explained this more carefully, events may have taken a different course. So in this case, *Mêtis* and *Epistêmê* lost that creative paradoxical relationship.

So far we have explored the nature of knowledge in how events might work out, for example in a workshop. But what about how the relationship between us as writers and you as reader also has an important bearing on knowledge and knowing? The ideas in this book are abstract, they are epistemic. To become useful and to affect your practice this will take reflection, probably conversation with others and further action. Here it is worth taking on board the words of Alfred North Whitehead (1866–1947), a widely influential philosopher and someone interested in the nature of process:

> You cannot think without abstractions, it is of the utmost importance to be vigilant in critically revising your modus of abstraction. It is here that philosophy finds its niche as essential to the healthy process of society. It is the critic of abstractions...

(Hernes, 2014, p.257)

He points to our natural tendency to understand, remember and converse that privileges abstraction; to do otherwise becomes too difficult. So the ideas of *Mêtis* and *Epistêmê* are just that, albeit with our efforts to contextualise them, you will go away with some sense of both as an abstract idea. But as Whitehead points out, although this is an important feature of knowing, it needs to be done with a sense of humility; these are not techniques that can be picked up and applied in any situation. It is therefore important to be critical of such ideas, but in doing so adapt, reflect and do the hard work of connecting these abstractions with your experience.

Implications for practice

What counts for knowledge is therefore rarely clear cut and is prone to shift in ways that often go unnoticed, both in terms knowledge itself and the assumptions or 'ground rules' that count for knowledge in that community. Knowledge exists in the patterns of relationships as people continuously make judgements about what to take seriously, how insights should be assimilated with others, whose opinion to believe and the allegiances one is willing to be associated with. Knowledge in the pattern of organisational relationships is political and laden with power.

At a macro scale, one can see this is different for different professional groupings: if you have worked with doctors in a hospital they have a view of knowledge that is different from creatives in an advertising agency. This should not come as a surprise, but these differences occur at the micro or nano scale: different teams, shared experiences of hard times and achievements, formative education, working at different sites, sports teams and so on. These differences can be surprising and made manifest in conflict that can occur unexpectedly. All of these add to what is taken seriously. The social constructionists Mary and Kenneth Gergen (Gergen and Gergen, 2008) make the point that a community forms a metatheory of knowledge, a way of interacting that is not consciously decided but is a cultural consensus as to what counts and what does not.

There are implications for OD both in terms of what counts for knowledge within our practice in the OD community and the communities in which we work.

- The act of asking questions from the perspective of the outsider causes moments of reflection and doubt as they come to explain what is obvious to them and therefore infrequently examined, but...
- Challenging conversations comes with risk. On the one hand, questions might be revealing and important in enabling reflexive understanding of self and community. They may form a useful challenge to unnoticed assumptions. But if they are too challenging, they can undermine a sense of identity and legitimacy that may have taken years to develop.
- When and how one goes about this matters too. The freedom to ask naïve and challenging questions shifts. Initially, one has licence to ask on the basis of being new, but this rapidly changes. Later on, one might obtain 'permission' to challenge on a basis of a knowledge chimera between acquired knowing of the community and what one brings from other experiences outside.
- So right from the first encounter, one is thus part of a knowledge network that is shifting; and that network now comprises us, the OD consultant. We too are affected.

How we think and use frameworks

There is a time, of course, when it is vital for us as practitioners for the context-free knowledge of *Epistêmê* and the context-bound knowledge of *Mêtis* to meet. That is when we are learning to use a tool or framework as part of our OD practice. At this time, it may be vital to understand the epistemic underpinnings of the framework, to learn where it originates and acknowledge the thinking of its originators. They may have had a good reason to suggest that a tool or framework be used in a particular way.

For example, when we first become interested in, say something like action learning, we may attend a course on the subject. Perhaps there is a requirement to develop a theoretical and historical understanding of action learning, followed by a practical assessment to obtain a qualification. As part of the practical we are given forms to fill in that mark out the action-learning process that we are to adopt. As we go through the practical, we may be very mindful to stick to the process that is expected of us, including such things as types of questions or timings. At this stage, totally imbued with epistemic learning, we may not pay much attention to the nature of the conversation we are having with the people in the action-learning set we are working with. We may hear what they say, but not be deeply listening, let alone making connections to get a wider perspective. In other words, the framework is a set of rules to be adhered to with the focus of attention being on those rules.

Roll forward through the years and the framework is still there but is now serving two different purposes, firstly for us and secondly for those we work with on action learning. The framework sits at the back of our mind, in our unconscious. When we get stuck, we might draw on the framework to help us to make the next move; for example, getting the participant to reframe their problem.

John Dewey, the US educationalist of the pragmatist school, points out: "Experience, in short, is not a combination of mind and world, subject and object, method and subject matter, but a single continuous interaction of a great diversity of energies" (Dewey, 2007, p.127). In offering examples from playing the piano he makes the point that there is no distinction between subject matter and method in a well-functioning activity, it becomes second nature. We start out in a technique like action learning anxious to 'do the right thing'. It is like an instruction manual, where we usefully consider experience in terms of 'right and wrong'. When we become more experienced facilitators, we think in terms of the relationship with people at that time and how it might be better in the context of their needs.

There are many frameworks and techniques in OD. These might be general (appreciative inquiry, action learning, action research and so on) or they may be covered by intellectual property protections, such as the European Foundation in Quality Management (EFQM). Either way they have an objective with a defined approach or methodology. Whilst it is vital to draw on the experience of the originator, often hard won, and see that experience as useful, epistemic knowledge, a framework can only ever be a shallow description and implies an untroubled context. By 'shallow description' we mean a technique described in a few bullet points or pages in a book which bears little resemblance to the situation as you walk into a room to carry out the task for the first time. When faced with a shifting context in which someone does or says somethings that throws them out of kilter, the experienced facilitator can draw on their *Mêtis* knowledge, their intuition to 'read the situation' and decide how next to act in relation to shifting and sometimes unsettling political dynamics.

Words can therefore only go so far. Ludwig Wittgenstein (1889–1951) was one of the most influential thinkers of the twentieth century and is relevant here. He was intrigued as to how ideas and words ironically get in the way of meaning, particularly philosophy, as to how people come to describe ordinary everyday activity. In a short book, *On Certainty*, written towards the end of his life he noted that:

> Not only rules, but also examples are needed for establishing a practice. Our rules leave loop-holes open, and the practice has to speak for itself.

> We do not learn the practice of making empirical judgements by learning rules: we are taught judgements and their connexion with other *judgements*. The *totality* of judgements is made plausible to us.

> When we first begin to believe anything, what we believe is not a single proposition, it is a whole system of propositions (light dawns gradually over the whole).

> (Wittgenstein, 1969, Para 139, 140 and 141)

Wittgenstein is pointing out that 'rules', or frameworks in this case, that have been captured and written down, can only go so far. However hard one tries to be clear, we will inevitably leave gaps between the carefully crafted words and what plays out in practice. Frameworks therefore have their place but they are limited.

At the start of this chapter, we began by discussing abstract facts and concepts (i.e. *Epistêmê*), but these are only useful if attention is paid to how we use this knowledge in relation to our intuition, built up over years, and the political process we are part of (i.e. *Mêtis*). In short, we need to give voice to both despite the problem that it is easier to talk of the former, issues of intuition and politics often being inaccessible not only to others but to ourselves too. Frameworks have the ability to form useful abbreviations in thought but can lead us to jump too readily to conclusions. The poet Robert Graves (1895–1985) drew attention to the problems of quick thinking when he wrote 'In Broken Images'. Here is the whole poem:

> He is quick, thinking in clear images;
> I am slow, thinking in broken images.
>
> He becomes dull, trusting to his clear images;
> I become sharp, mistrusting my broken images.
>
> Trusting his images, he assumes their relevance;
> Mistrusting my images, I question their relevance.
>
> Assuming their relevance, he assumes the fact;
> Questioning their relevance, I question the fact.
>
> When the fact fails him, he questions his senses;
> When the fact fails me, I approve my senses.
>
> He continues quick and dull in his clear images;
> I continue slow and sharp in my broken images.
>
> He in a new confusion of his understanding;
> I in a new understanding of my confusion.

The questions this chapter invites

- In an age of information and machine learning, what sort of human knowledge is now valued?
- How does this affect people's access to continuous professional and personal development?
- What does a learning organisation look like now?
- How relevant are training programmes now? Do coaching, action learning and technologically enabled learning meet current needs more effectively?

Abstract knowledge and facts still have their place but this is becoming increasingly less the case as they are now readily at our finger tips and machines have come to learn, adapt and interpret. However, contextual forms of knowledge and learning in terms of *Mêtis* are increasingly important in this rapidly shifting world in which we interact with both machines and people.

You may want to consider your own practice carefully. How would you explain to your younger self what you do and what others value in you? Better still, what improvements can you make and what new interfaces will be required (such as different people, cultures, machines that learn)? Consider a situation in which you became vividly aware of your emotions, your visceral reaction, and the interaction between this and your detached logical self. How did you make sense of and understand the choices you made? What was the nature of that hyper sense of awareness? And from this, what ideas and concepts enabled you to go forward? In short, how would you describe your knowledge, learning and knowing in a way that gives voice to you as a person, a person of logic and thought as well as emotion and physiological response, particularly as you work with others in an unknown situation?

Photo: © Steve Marshall, www.drstevemarshall.com, @drstevemarshall

Artful practice to inspire human systems

Introduction

IF LEARNING AS WE have talked about it is a contingent and context-specific activity, then the question we ask is how can we learn whilst paying attention to our whole being, using what John Heron and Peter Reason call the "wider ways of knowing"? This is a broader epistemology (theory of knowledge) that isn't limited to what we 'know in our heads' but respects our embodied, emotional, psychic and even spiritual selves; that is, it pays attention to our deeply artful nature (Heron and Reason, 2008).

Art is striking in its pervasiveness. It is an essential quality of being a person and of being with others. The evidence stretches back millennia, to a time long before writing. Even today where survival is at risk and people are in the direst of circumstances, they turn to art. In organisations, conversations about art and its close companions, imagination and creativity, are largely absent or only whispered, even if they are hankered after as some kind of grail of competitive edge. When we look back on success, a notable marketing campaign, medical breakthrough or a novel computing algorithm, artistry is at work. This relates not only to the genesis of the idea but also to how people come to work together to bring it to fruition. Artistry has many aspects.

What if organisations were places of artistry where people were creative, bringing the entirety of themselves to their work? By this we mean more than their intellectual, technical and fine motor skills and muscular selves, or whatever else is emphasised in a job description. What might be the impact on the wider canvas of the organisation? Artistry in this context belongs to us all and is made manifest in the progress we make together. We therefore reject the notion of the artist being a highly gifted individual holed up in their garret producing beautiful objects; it resides in all of us.

What then for the organisational development practitioner? It is an artistry of bringing the artist out in others. We are talking of new connections, of seeing the world differently, of developing confidence and of risk. The OD practitioner is a bringer of new ideas, an organisational traveller; it is an 'in-between' role – wanted, needed but not always fully trusted.

In this chapter we explore what artistry might mean for the OD practitioner and what we might usefully notice and explore, not about completed art but in the dynamics of its creation – because that is all we have. We provide a few broad outlines and illustrations, not an exhaustive list.

Being artful: heritage and implications

"In the absence of more money, the NHS will need more imagination..."

(*Economist*, 2017)

Figure 4.1: Cave paintings at Chauvet, France: evidence of humans organising together and being artful

For as long as humanity has existed, we seem to have had an urge to create. Some of the earliest artefacts of human organising, the cave paintings at Chauvet, France (See Figure 4.1), were drawn on stone in the most inaccessible reaches of the cave system. Not only does this demonstrate artistry and ingenuity, it also gives an indication of how much did not survive. Palaeontologists define the approximately 100,000-year-long existence of the modern human mind in terms of these artefacts. These works suggest that survival, community and artistry were interracially woven.

Ben Okri, the Nigerian author, talks about humanity being the species *homo fabula*, the people who tells stories. Could we also be described as *homo fabrica*, those who make? We have always made with our hands and our minds; and later, with the help of pictographic and then abstract language, have transmitted our artful selves far and wide. With the help of radio transmission and space exploration, that artful expression now even resides beyond our own solar system, for example, in the form of the Voyager space probes, launched in 1979. Despite this, we have developed an ability to subdue our artistic side, favouring instead the rationality of the spreadsheet. It is our role in OD to find ways to honour that innate capacity, not just because it is there, but because it may be essential to the creation of human and organisational flourishing. And to meet the very real challenge with which we started this chapter.

Yuri Slezkine, of the University of California, Berkeley, talks about two fundamental groupings in society, which we can extend to the organisations we create (Slezkine, 2004). He calls them Mercurians and Apollonians. The Mercurians (from Mercury, the messenger) represent the artful, storytelling capacities that operate between the settlements and villages (or should we say, in organisations, departments) of Apollo's realm. The Apollonians are rooted to the land; the Mercurians are connected by stories and practices of service. Slezkine also calls the Mercurians 'service nomads', more connected by a mindset than a geographical location. They travel from town to town, providing itinerant labour, special services, such as knife sharpening, exotic goods and sometimes entertainment. There exists a tension between these two interdependent groups. It isn't altogether an easy relationship. But they need each other: the Apollonians produce the food, but the Mercurians provide the flavour. Indeed, spice merchants are a good historical example of Mercurians.

The Mercurian's role illustrates a perennial human character. They embody an 'artful' quality. If we assume that OD practitioners are the modern organisational Mercurians, then the source of our creativity is our difference, our uniqueness, our story and how we embody and express it through our imaginal capacity. John Heron defines this imaginal capacity as:

> the capacity of the psyche to generate an individual viewpoint, a unique outlook on life through the use of imagery – in sense perception, memory, anticipation, dreams, visions, imagination, extrasensory perception. Such imagery yields a distinctive, personal window on the world.

(Heron, 1992, p.17)

Organisations that seek innovation, creativity, productivity, the 'discretionary effort' that gives them an edge may not realise it, but what they need is a direct output of the artful and imaginative process. Our capacity to create potentially comes from our artfulness and this includes almost every task we undertake, even the most mundane, essentially as long as we emotionally own what we do. It is quite possible to imagine that when the art of our labour is fully outsourced, on a factory production line, for example, then perhaps this artfulness disappears. But it is noticeable that even in factories, some effort has been made to put the artfulness back in, for example in the Kaisen 'quality circles' of automotive production originating in Japan.

For the OD practitioner, this artful capacity is at the root of our difference; it's what makes us special, gives us the ability to engage in useful ways with the systems we are working with. By knowing and articulating our ongoing story, we can help to tell the story of the organisation and this can be powerful and transformative.

As practitioners, we are organisational troubadours with knowledge of other lands, of colour and intrigue. We are often treated with caution but nonetheless as possessing the ability to make connections and incite new ways of looking at the world. It is a role mixed with opportunity and responsibility.

An artful invitation

This chapter contains an incitement to your own artfulness and that of the clients you serve. Heron's definition of the imaginal is partial: it is more than just a visual capacity, it is also embodied, smelt, felt, tasted, heard and touched. You may approach the concept of artfulness with trepidation, thinking to yourself, "I am not artful, I can't draw, paint, or sing". But perhaps you can cook, organise an excellent efficient project or tell a good story. You have a family history that provides many stories of colour. You have a capacity to dream, by night and day. You can usefully let your mind wander as you stare out of the window, finding faces in the clouds. The way you express this artfulness may be unique to you. And you can also express this by how you practise change at work, as Franck explains:

> I know artists whose medium is Life itself, and who express the inexpressible without brush, pencil, chisel or guitar. They neither paint nor dance. Their medium is Being. Whatever their hand touches has increased Life. They SEE and don't have to draw. They are the artists of being alive.

> (Franck, 1973)

Artfulness isn't about being an artist in the narrow sense. Indeed, it is a symptom of the challenge we face that art has become ghettoised as a series of professions or the hobbies that we do outside of work. Maybe our role is to re-inspire ourselves and our organisations with an artful spirit, as "artists of being alive", as Franck says. Your skill may be in something that you never imagined would be defined as artful. Like the way you listen, build relationships, work with a team, help your child with their school project or even how you ride a motorcycle.

Henry Mintzberg, the Canadian strategist, tells a story that illustrates the power of this narrative, as it sits in the DNA of the Honda motor company. He describes how an unintentional practice became a sales strategy, which became a marketing campaign, which became a corporate legend. It was to do with this Japanese company's approach to the sale of motorbikes in the US market in the 1950s and '60s. With targets to sell larger-engined bikes (which had a greater margin), the salespeople travelled around Los Angeles, so the story goes, on the small 50cc cubs that Honda never thought would be of interest to a US market. But these are the ones that caught the eye of the dealers. Mintzberg explains:

> In 1959, Honda, a Japanese manufacturer of motorcycles, not (yet) automobiles, entered the American market. By 1966, it had 63 percent of that market.

> (Mintzberg et al., 2005)

It was the motorbike dealers' experience of these young, charming Japanese salesmen, zooming around the city on their little cub motorbikes, that lead to the slogan Honda used as part of its American marketing campaign: "You meet the nicest people on a Honda".

We can see artfulness in so many aspects of this story. We see it in the way these sales people beguiled their American customers. We see it in the quality of the little motorbikes that the company's founder, Sochiro Honda, had lovingly perfected in his post-war garage. We also see it in the marketing campaign that evoked the experience of this relationship that emerged on the streets of LA. We see it in how the story represented a *difference* – clean-cut young men riding cute little cub motorbikes was a refreshing contrast to the leather-clad, macho male preserve. In the public's imagination, it could be something that 'nice' people do. And perhaps above all, we see it in how the story itself emerged, galvanised the company, and how the narrative still lurks at the core of its soul and influences even contemporary choices it makes. This suggests an artistry from a different angle, an artistry of self that adapts and flexes to new opportunities. Perhaps this is also what is meant by self as instrument? Members of *homo fabrica* create their own identity. This can be in the service of business, organisations or a wider social purpose. Our artfulness suggests that we always ask deeper ethical questions about what our making is in service of. Richard Sennett discusses this in his contemplation of the craft exhibited by the group of scientists, led by J. Robert Oppenheimer, who fabricated the first atomic weapons:

> Craftsmanship is certainly, from an ethical point of view, ambiguous. Robert Oppenheimer was a committed craftsman; he pushed his technical skills to the limit to make the best bomb he could. ... The good craftsman, moreover, uses solutions to uncover new territory; problem solving and problem finding are intimately related in his or her mind. For this reason, curiosity can ask "Why?" as well as, "How?" about any project. The craftsman thus both stands in Pandora's shadow and can step out of it.

> (Sennett, 2008, p.11)

Sennett is inviting us to recognise that our artful choices are always ethical choices by illustrating how our creativity often opens the Pandora's box of unintended consequences, just as the story of these young Japanese salesmen shows us. Of course, it is only a story, and such corporate myths abound. It may be a different discussion to consider the veracity of these accounts. Did this really happen? Or at least, did it happen in this way? (One lesser-told version of the story, according to Mintzberg, is that the sales people were forced to sell the smaller bikes because the larger ones, unsuited to the long distances travelled in the US compared to Japan, kept breaking down!) True or not, this shows us that our artful nature is powerful, more powerful perhaps than simple (and sometimes inconvenient) facts, which can be usefully ignored in support of what we want to believe. This raises other ethical questions, of course, which we address elsewhere (see Chapter 6). Nevertheless, this demon-strates the yearning of people for a galvanising and transformative story, a yearning to connect with the artful. That is where the OD practitioner's work starts. It is our opportunity.

We suggest that there is a particular urgency for artfulness in organisations. In both the public and private sectors, a particular kind of ceiling has been met where the rational, hierarchical control-based cultures of the corporate mainstream are falling to deliver the required improvement, particularly as systems and markets become ever-more complex and globalised.

Consider the pharmaceutical industry. Mark Kessel, writing in the journal *Nature Biotechnology* in 2011, put the situation bluntly:

> Is there any doubt that the leading drug companies are in desperate need of reinvention? Blockbuster drugs are coming off patent or being taken off the market for safety reasons and there are no replacement drugs on the horizon to make up the shortfall in profits. Furthermore, healthcare reform is likely to exacerbate the flaws in big pharma's traditional business model by imposing pay for performance, as is already the case in Europe. To state the obvious, over the past decade, the pharmaceutical industry has brought few drugs to market from its own development efforts. Commentators have stressed, and heads of

big pharma have acknowledged, that the sector's R&D [research and development] efforts need to be drastically changed.

(Kessel, 2011)

Could it be that part of the challenge here is rooted in a culture that doesn't know how to be artful? As Albert Einstein apparently said: "If you always do as you've always done, then you'll always get what you've always got". Organisations like big pharma companies have rationalised, focused on profitability, audited themselves to within an inch of their lives, and from this instrumental stance, the Muses (the Greek Goddesses who preside over creative inspiration) have been ignored. August Kekulé, the nineteenth-century chemist and inventor of benzene, claimed he was inspired to synthesise its ring-like structure when he had a dream of a snake seizing its own tail. Even chemistry needs artful inspiration.

So being artful in an OD context may be about a more fundamental move than organising executive playdates with crayons. As Seeley and Thornhill put it:

> We advocate for consciously bringing fuller, more-than-intellectual ways of knowing into the workplace and for using these to reshape the fundamental ways business is structured.

(Seeley and Thornhill, 2014)

At the core of artful expression is often some working out of our stories; the transmutation of which defines the course of our artful inquiry. What is the link between your story and what you do? Is it a coincidence that a person whose life was saved by the NHS devotes their life to improving the quality of patient care? Or that someone with a rare genetic anomaly becomes a world-leading geneticist? Or that the youngest child of a large family becomes an OD practitioner, to figure out the human dynamics that often bemused them in their family as a child? These questions acknowledge the deeply rooted nature of our artfulness. They aren't about some kind of pathological drive; it is more to do with how we differentiate ourselves and devote our energy to crafting ourselves whilst crafting some change in the world.

In this section, we have tested the definition of the artist beyond the expert in their studio. We all have abilities and we can all develop confidence in our artistry. How we engage with our imagination and spark the imagination of others are crucial in our artistry and will enable us to respond to many of the challenges we face. The question that we now address concerns what we might do to enable this.

Artfulness in the work of the OD practitioner

What follows is not a comprehensive list but rather an offering of what might be possible and relevant for you. We hope that you will see connections between these ideas and your own practice and develop the confidence to explore and try some ideas for yourself. Like the Mercurians, we hope to provide some flavour.

Transmutation

Here James explains:

> For a few months now I have been living with a trapped nerve in my shoulder. It isn't overly painful now, although it was when it first became figural for me, after a four-hour drive through France on our way home from a family holiday. It mainly manifests itself now with numbness in my fingers and occasionally, when I am tired or cold, with pains in my wrists, elbow and shoulder. I have tried many things in the service of treatment. Painkillers, MRI scans and visits to a specialist neurosurgeon were part of the traditional medical offering. Surgery too is an option but even the neurosurgeon himself didn't seem too keen to slice into the back of my neck. For this I was grateful. I also regularly visited a hardworking osteopath, who gave a whole new meaning to the words 'hands on'. I screamed so loud we ended up in a giggling heap as he contemplated his apology to the next customer in the waiting room. He and the neurosurgeon both recommended exercise, activity, swimming in particular, which was music to my ears, as I love to swim. What I seem to have though is a persistent level of symptoms that are manageable enough. My sleep isn't disturbed anymore and the occasional pins and needles are no more than annoying.

> But something else has been going on, I notice. It is a kind of conversation with this shoulder pain – a kind of archetypal discourse that has emerged in the months since it arrived. I notice I have personified it. It has a character. I talk to it. It has become like an irritating companion but oddly not an altogether unwelcome one (and I know that sounds strange). It is a bit like the volley ball, Wilson, that Tom Hanks befriends in the film *Castaway*. Don't get me wrong. I am sure that I would be better off without it, but meanwhile, I have come to accommodate it and it has developed a life alongside me, which isn't altogether unproductive. I notice how it has made me contemplate my health, exercise more, pay attention to my posture and appreciate the good things in life. When I hear the stories of people who have much more serious ailments, I am chastened. It may sound weird but my pain in the neck has become a kind of mentor.

This illustrates what artfulness might be, both for people as individuals and working together in organisations. If we see the pain in the neck as the metaphor, it could be considered an entirely different mindset with which to approach the troublesome parts of the organisation that don't fit the current status quo. It suggests that our role as OD people in an organisation is to move towards, embrace and galvanise, or even transmute, these challenges. Our role is to make the pain in the neck useful to the whole 'corporation' (a word which derives from 'body'). It is something we all do: transmute the mundane into something quite wonderful, or at least developmental and interesting, as a core function of the collective human mind.

People in concentration camps painted, drew, made music. They even took part in boxing matches. They did this even though it put them in more peril, being forbidden. Imagine the creativity that went into organising a secret boxing match in a concentration camp. Homo fabrica indeed. The artful expression of self is a vital part of human salvation, the transmutation of the horrifying, or even just the mundane, the composting of what appears to us to be waste into fertile soil.

> How might our lives and organisations evolve in ways that are neither reduced to doom and gloom hair-shirt narratives of 'less', nor reliant on the unrealistic mantra of business-as-usual-because-technology-will-save-us?

(Seeley and Thornhill, 2014)

The art of restoring relationships – an example

A good example of artfully moving towards the difficult was the work we have done in Restorative Practice, an approach to HR and OD that deliberately aims to transmute the challenges of an organisation into its gold. The programme was a two-year collaboration with a local authority, within which it was successfully used as an effective first response to workplace grievances and performance improvements. It was inspired by restorative justice principles. It represented a brave move for an organisation mired in bureaucratic approaches, developing staff so they can help to resolve differences and disputes more personally, rather than using a formal route. Advantages included increased motivation, reduced numbers of formal grievances and, perhaps most significantly, staff feedback surveys showing that people felt they had been treated with dignity. A memorable example was the way one particular practitioner artfully dealt with a highly complex issue. This was a complex set of relationships in a school, involving a longstanding staff member who was struggling with alcoholism. This popular character was taking increasingly lengthy bouts of absence. The school leadership wanted it dealt with. The restorative practitioner who was brought in had to work skilfully with a number of complex structures and relationships: for example, the person in question, although very much part of the school community, wasn't formally employed by the school but by a third-party agency. It was a contractual minefield and everyone was understandably avoiding facing these complexities.

A number of qualities mark out the practitioner's approach: they had no agenda, apart from being of service to the system; they admitted they didn't have an 'answer'; they moved towards facilitating dialogue; and above all, they became, in their words, a "space of listening". Ultimately, the member of staff in question was enabled to seek help and the quality of relationships was enhanced; and in the words of the practitioner, the "community wasn't harmed in dealing with this." In fact, as the restorative practitioner explained, there was a point where the opposite of harm was achieved. By moving towards the difficult, a kind of transmutation was achieved:

> I brought together the head teacher, the person and their manager. The four of us sat down together. It was awkward at first, but I managed to get each one of them to talk about what was going on from their own point of view. The person in question said at one point. "I didn't realise it was affecting everyone else so badly!" It prompted them to get some help. The head teacher also felt like she had got something off her chest. Whilst we didn't turn it into a holiday camp, there was a sense that things weren't just resolved; that everyone had got something slightly better out of the difficulty of it all.

The art here was in the skills of dialogue, which have the potential to transmute broken relationships into productive and trusting ones.

The art of speaking truth to power

How can OD work artfully with power? One of the finest expressions of the possibilities artfulness affords us is the use of what James C. Scott calls the "hidden transcript":

> If subordinate discourse in the presence of the dominant is a public transcript, I shall use the term 'hidden transcript' to characterise discourse that takes place 'offstage', beyond direct observation by powerholders.

(Scott, 1990, p.4)

Simply put, the hidden transcript is a way that less powerful people in any human system cleverly play the game. Our role in OD might be to create, through artful means, some kind of meeting between those public and hidden transcripts. The example that James Scott uses is how African slaves in the Southern states of the US used Christianity to critique their enslavement in a sophisticated way that their white slave owners couldn't object to. After all, if they were singing about being liberated from Babylon one fine day, it was the biblical one they were referring to, wasn't it?

So how does that relate to our work in organisations? These slaves were artfully creating the stage for meaning but in a way that is mindful of the power dynamics and keeping 'face' for participants, or the powerful. A slave owner who loses face becomes highly dangerous; a chief executive who loses face perhaps offers less physical peril but nonetheless, this might be a situation better avoided. But to speak truth to power, there may need to be the expression of a hidden transcript. On the one hand, there does need to be movement of those relations but, on the other, not so much that they fracture. It is a dynamic negotiation of risk (with opportunity and damage constantly present). This is a great example of how hidden transcripts have always operated, enabling a kind of rebellion that is safer to conduct for those who may risk suffering from a more overt one. It is a wonderful expression of artfulness.

The art here is in helping to bring these hidden transcripts out, in a way that minimises the risk of reproach or punishment, but which enables those in more powerful positions (which may not be those at the top of the organisation) to catch a glimpse of what may be hidden to them. Much of the bread-and-butter work of OD is in the careful management of messages across power lines. Contracting for confidentiality in a team discussion or action-learning set, for example, is about enabling the expression of the hidden transcripts. Another example is the taking of some of the 'data' collected in the early phase of a piece of OD diagnostic work and holding it up to the senior sponsor in a way that they can hear.

There is a particular art to this. As T.S. Eliot wrote, "Humankind cannot bear very much reality". So the judicious choices, careful phrasing, artful negotiation and moulding of forms of feedback are all highly artful processes.

If you consider the classic 'iceberg' model of human systems, as devised by Edgar Schein, the art of reading the relevant dynamics under the 'surface' of everyday socialised human behaviour is probably one of the most vital qualities of OD work. What does this art comprise? It requires:
- Self-awareness
- Empathy
- Subtle reading
- Emotional intelligence
- Systemic thinking
- Timing.

John Shotter summarises this type of artfulness as "with-ness thinking":

> How, as any kind of practitioner, do we recognise what the material of our practice is, how to move about within it, and how to choose with any surety what it seems best to do in a particular situation before us?

(Shotter, 2005, p.132)

Shotter borrows Goethe's term 'delicate empiricism' to explain with-ness capacity. It is more than a rational ability; in fact it is quite different from the normal capacity to 'think about' a situation from the observer's vantage point. Instead, he stresses a lived involvement from within which we develop a tuned perception of events. He points out:

> What we can gain in our understandings-from-within, is a subsidiary awareness... of certain 'action guiding feelings' that can play a role in giving us an anticipatory sense of at least the style or the grammar of what is to come next in the ongoing process in which we happen to be involved, feelings which are lost in descriptions 'from the outside'...

(Shotter, 2005, p.585)

It requires us to sense the world as being an ongoing connected wholeness that is beyond spatial atomic units. It is a kind of expression; that is, essentially artful:

> there is a 'poetic' way of talking and writing here – what we might call 'with-ness' – writing... within which we can express what we find in our criss-cross journeyings over these often befogged landscapes. Ways of talking and writing that... can 'point to' what next to expect out in the world of our everyday, practical affairs.

(Shotter, 2005, p.154)

Shotter isn't necessarily talking directly about poetry here but the poetic response to complex human relations. This is about how we make meaning in artful ways, one that beguiles and seduces the powerful and powerless to cross the invisible boundary that separates them most of the time in everyday organisational life. This is the role of the OD practitioner, to find artful, with-ness ways of managing power dynamics, so that truths can be expressed, understood and used for better decision making.

Sometimes the hidden transcript is structurally bound, in the way that organisations communicate, as much as in what is communicated. Here the art of speaking truth to power is expressed in the careful juggling of the dynamics in a system. Leadership teams often have to go through certain rituals and the artful OD practitioner needs to work alongside them in order to facilitate change. A development director of a US-based education institute brought this home, as James explains:

> I had to present a business case to the Finance Committee of the school for a big uplift in the investment in alumni relations, communications and development. Essentially, I had to demonstrate how the investment I was asking for would lead to them successfully raising $100m in 10 years' time. So I built the mother of all spreadsheets, which I then presented to the Leadership Team, and we spent an hour with them interrogating my assumptions and dependencies. Their decision was approved.
>
> However, I knew that raising large sums from relatively small numbers of potential donors is unpredictable and doesn't submit to being modelled in this way. Moreover, the people on whom we would be counting to make the most significant gifts were the very people with whom I was talking, along with their Board colleagues! I think in their heart of hearts they knew this too, but we had to go through the motions of making what was in fact an intensely political and relational process look 'sciencey' and data driven.
>
> Although the spreadsheet was 'made up', we successfully raised £100m. It took twelve years rather than ten and there were many curves and twists in the road along the way that we could never have predicted back when we made the business case; but certainly, without that original investment decision, the money would never have been raised.

There could be a number of interpretations of what is going on here. At one level, it could be that the spreadsheet was a form of social object, as described by the American pragmatist philosopher George H. Mead (Mead, 1934), around which people's attention could be gathered. Work was done in kicking around assumptions and gradually moving towards commitment. One would not be able to move towards this without an object of some sort. Karl Weick retells a story about a group of soldiers on an Alpine journey who found their way by following a map. The trouble was, it wasn't a map of where they were. Yet having a map provided them with a sense of cohesion and direction that ultimately saved them (Weick, 1995).

Another interpretation is that decision-making processes at senior levels in organisations are more like rituals than the rational data-weighing routines they pretend to be. In which case, the role of the practitioner is to become an artful choreographer of the dance of these relationships.

There may be other interpretations, yet they all seem to point to the possibilities of artfulness as a way of facilitating the truth telling required for organisational flourishing. The example below illustrates this further.

Using forum theatre to explore gender in a police context – an example

We practised an example of playing the hidden transcript back to the organisation when we were working within a UK police constabulary around its 'gender agenda' – improving the quality of equality across the workforce in both 'civilian' and 'police' staff (to use their terminology).

We were aware that there was a lot of cynicism around the type of initiatives that had been launched over the years to address these issues. Our task was to organise a big event at which the subject could be explored in a playful and explorative fashion. We had done some action research and wanted to play back the results to a gathered group of about 150 identified opinion formers drawn from all ranks and across the service. We decided to create a series of 'plays' that showed some of the behaviours that we had uncovered in the research, around gender, as the main menu for the day. We recognised that we needed to engage artfully with some of the hidden transcripts that abounded. Although people would pay lip service to the issues, we knew that they still prevailed. So how would we craft a way of surfacing these safely and thoughtfully without making people feel bad?

The solution we hit upon was to use the messy start of a conference to our advantage. We decided to place two actors, a man and a woman in the audience of the auditorium, and have them conduct a conversation. They would be connected to microphones, so people could hear the conversation as they walked into the auditorium. The conversation went along the lines of what we had heard in the research; it was a playback of the hidden transcripts, a sceptical dialogue about "pointless corporate events that don't help the ordinary copper (as they called themselves) to do their work." As this broadcasted conversation progressed, a camera settled upon the two actors, who found themselves seats together in the front row, and they were shown on the large screens as they continued their discussion. The rest of the audience started to catch on and laughter bubbled around the hall. People from right across the hierarchy, from the highest ranking officers to the probationary constables caught the fact that their own sceptical hidden transcript was being played back to them.

This opened up people's willingness to engage with the rest of the event. The hidden transcript had in some way been usefully exposed.

Artful choreography

Artful knowing encompasses receiving experience, ideas, data and responding in arts-enriched ways – it is not an analytical, rational thought process but an active doing process.

(Seeley and Thornhill, 2014)

A practitioner of storytelling in community development, a woman called Theresa Holden*, once taught a group of us a storytelling-as-research process. The idea was that you get people to tell short 'I was there' vignettes based on a theme and using the sensory details they'd encountered. From this, you could deduce the real, experienced truths around themes such as community, leadership and engagement. One of the things she was staunch about was getting people to sit in a circle. "It has to be a good circle", she would say. "The quality of the stories people tell is directly proportional to the quality of listening you create, and that in turn requires a really good circle".

It is deceptively simple how the space a group sits in has a profound impact on the quality of the dialogue that ensues. As a practitioner, we may usefully pay great attention to the simple rules of creating a convivial environment in which a group can have effective conversations. There is an art to it. Toke Paludan Moeller, the Dutch OD specialist, calls this the "art of hosting".

It is slightly shocking to think that, perhaps when working with a very senior team of people, the simple hygiene factors of the room they are in, as well as the quality of the air and the coffee, have an impact on their state of mind and thereby the efficacy of multi-million-pound decision making. Yet it is as true for them as for anyone else. There is an art to staging good quality organisational work, making sure the environment is convivial, or that people are not hungry or bursting for the toilet and it is likely to be the OD practitioner who pays attention to this when everyone else may be overlooking it.

Research bears this out. In the US, the esteemed National Academy of Science published a paper in 2011 that showed that the likelihood of prisoners being granted parole dropped significantly when the sitting panel's blood sugar was low.

> We find that the percentage of favorable rulings drops gradually from ≈65% to nearly zero within each decision session and returns abruptly to ≈65% after a break. Our findings suggest that judicial rulings can be swayed by extraneous variables that should have no bearing on legal decisions.
>
> (Raymer et al., 2014)

This may be shocking, but it suggests that in good quality human decision making, there is a requirement for an artful choreography of relationships. There are all sorts of ways in which the OD professional might artfully manage the quality of an environment in their work, from the depths of human expression and contact to the most banal issues of room layout and furniture.

---

* See www.holdenarts.org

OD practitioners who have a dry patch could always go into furniture removals. They are practised at it because they usually find that they have to reorganise any room they have been given, to make it more convivial for dialogue. Is there a big boardroom table that creates immovable distance between participants? Has the hotel venue, which was asked to set up the room 'cabaret style' with groups of chairs, set up the large banqueting tables so that the intimacy you had hoped to create is dissipated amongst a group of ten who can hardly hear each other, let alone share experiences? Are there empty chairs in a circle? (A colleague of ours used to call these "hungry ghost chairs" because they attracted symbolic presences into the room.) Sometimes of course, it may be that you deliberately place empty chairs in a group in order to signify the voices of people, customers, other staff groups and so on whose voices and presence you want to invoke.

James continues:

> Years ago, in a previous life, I worked in the theatre as a stage manager. It always amazed me how, with a few sheets of hardboard, a bit of paint, lots of thick sticky tape and clever lighting, we were able to quickly evoke any kind of environment and its consequent mood. It strikes me that people are quite malleable in this sense, and of course that raises ethical questions about our purpose when we are working in this way. But I fall back on the etymological derivation of the word 'facilitation', which means 'to make things easy'.

Artful stage management, the choreography of groups who are 'eased' into a more effective set of conversations is thus a legitimate part of our role; it creates the right sort of environment for the purpose we are trying to achieve.

Going to church?

Sometimes, the environment we find ourselves in as practitioners can have unintended consequences, and the choreography and artistry are about working with 'what is'. We were running an event as part of an OD development programme for a group of internal HRBPs in a local authority. Early on in our work with the group, we hit a bit of a barrier. The group were keen to work but hadn't previously been exposed to some of the more advanced ideas around such things as 'parallel process' (the way in which some of the experiences in the organisation show up in the experience of participants in the here and now) or 'self as instrument' (how one's own make up and story can be instrumental in the work we do, creating an organising meaning to our work, helping us to define how we notice what we notice). But we found it hard to explain how these concepts worked in the abstract and some of the group struggled to understand them.

James reflects on the constraints of running a workshop and its impact:

> Due to challenging budget constraints, the local authority we were
> working with had struggled to find an affordable venue and it so
> happened that we found ourselves working in a church, because that
> was all that could be found. Coming from a Jewish background myself, I
> noticed I was feeling slightly uncomfortable about this setting. It was a
> lovely, airy and light modern building (as, ironically, we had clearly
> specified) but the iconography made me feel slightly uncomfortable.
> During our somewhat tangled conversations about these abstract
> concepts, I owned up to my discomfort. "That's myself as instrument
> showing up" I explained. "Being Jewish is an important part of it, as it
> locates me and provides a defining direction, a set of goggles that I see
> through in my practice." Once I said that, others (for example, a woman
> from a Muslim background) also admitted that they hadn't quite
> noticed but, now it had been mentioned, they also felt a response to
> being in that environment.

It wasn't necessarily uncomfortable for everyone but pretty much everyone
had a response of some sort or another. In fact, nearly everyone in the room
(Christians and non-Christians alike) admitted that the environment was having
some powerful yet 'under the radar' impact on them. This was a great illus-
tration of our diverse selves as instruments but it also threw into the foreground
issues of diversity. Once we had scratched the surface, we found significant,
profound and above all useful differences in our own group. "Ah! That's a
parallel process then!" said one of the participants. If we hadn't found ourselves
in a church and artfully worked with it, we might never have found ourselves at
all.

The dynamics of artful OD

By way of bringing this part of our exposition of artfulness to a close, we offer
an account from Rob that we think draws together threads of artful practice in
OD. In weaving these threads, one is artfully creating the stage for conversations and meaning to be had but in a way that is mindful of the power dynamics
and that allows participants to maintain 'face'. On the one hand, there does
need to be movement in those relations (otherwise, what change are we
effecting?); but on the other, not so much movement that they fracture. It is a
dynamic negotiation of risk, with opportunity and damage constantly present.
Here is a narrative of a meeting that offers a glimpse of the warp and weft of
this material.

Rob explains:

> I was asked to chair a workshop, a high-profile consultation exercise for
> a group of senior nurses who were transferring their employment to a

national body as part of a high-profile health initiative. My role included introducing the event, summing up at the end and making sure the event kept to time and achieved its objectives. In summary, I was to act as host and facilitator. I was concerned about the numbers attending the workshop and due to some clerical over-booking, we were expecting about seventy people, which I felt was far too many.

This particular workshop, one of a series, was held in London. In the question and answer session in the afternoon, my role was to field questions between the participants and a panel of directors and others who had been working on this particular area of work. I felt like the lightning conductor between the two groups. As a result, I was in a unique position to experience how people interacted.

I had felt the tension building up to this point for a couple of hours. The nurses were desperate to see the details of how it was envisaged that they would be working in the future. Over the previous few months, job descriptions had been developed, including the likely pay banding and some of the detail of their new working practices. I had lobbied for the job descriptions to be sent around before the workshop so there would not be too many surprises. This idea was rejected on the basis that some people were wary of giving the impression that too much work had been done before the event; bearing in mind that the event was aimed at getting their ideas on how the new service should be shaped. However, they would have known that the work had been done. The idea was even mooted of adding a few spelling mistakes to give the impression that the job descriptions were recently drafted and in an unfinished state, an issue that I felt uneasy about because it added to the deception.

At the beginning of the Q&A session, I experienced a flood of emotional anxiety aimed at me as facilitator, anxiety focused on why the job descriptions had not been sent out before and what was being hidden. I felt alive, in the moment of the experience. The fight-or-flight reflex brought a sense of sharpness and acuteness for me. I felt determined to stay with this experience through the course of the event. Although the anxiety subsided on handing out the job descriptions, the vibrancy of the experience continued. What I find interesting, as I write this, is that I can still feel that sense of energy, energy that I had felt to be absent during the meetings on planning that preceded the event. During the workshop I was aware of how the questions developed and were built upon by others in the room, how some points kept coming up time and time again, whilst others emerged and faded away, and also how the conversation often focused around a few vocal individuals.

During this, whilst acting like a lightning rod between the nurses and the directors and others, I noticed a shift. At the start, those with the upper hand, in terms of seniority within the organisation, appeared confident in presenting their view of the future. The projected slides were accompanied with polished explanations of how things would be. However, it was in the question and answer section that I noticed how control shifted and flexed throughout the room. I don't pretend that the way I facilitated this was as expert as it might have been; but I noticed how, in that facilitator role, we experience the possibility of artful movement of a dynamic in a system. It is unpredictable and dynamic, and there is both risk and opportunity alive in the moment of creativity.

The last word belongs to our friend and colleague Chris Seeley (1966–2014), one of the most artful of practitioners, who was committed to the end to the possibilities of artful expression in human systems.

> Artful practice co-operates at many different depths in organisational life, ranging from entertainment and decoration, through to propping up business-as-usual, through to skills training, and through to fundamentally questioning organisational purpose, structure and form. The movement between these different states can be fluid and unpredictable, unthinking and accidental or deeply conscious and mindful.

(Seeley and Thornhill, 2014)

The questions this chapter invites

- Given that the nature of work has changed markedly from what it was thirty years ago, what has been the impact on the human imagination?
- How has the investment in human imagination at work changed over the last thirty years?
- How has the role of the Mercurian changed and what are the territories the Apollonian now claims as their own?
- How different is the task of speaking truth to power now?

In this chapter, we sought to broaden what we might think of as art and to extend it to our practice as OD professionals, and to advocate for the task of recognising and encouraging artistry in others. Art in this sense is not just the creation of beautiful objects by the talented few; it extends to the way we do our daily work, at home and beyond, and what we see in others on the broadest of canvases. To meet the challenges of the future, new and imaginative ways of working will be essential. In the next chapter, we consider how we turn this essential artfulness towards crafting a meaningful strategy in our OD work.

Photo: © Steve Marshall, www.drstevemarshall.com, @drstevemarshall

5

Crafting an OD strategy

Introduction

I N THE PREVIOUS CHAPTER, we talked about being artful and its impact across the canvas of the organisation. What then are the implications for the individual as they develop their craft? A tool can only work in the hands of a person experienced in their craft and it is this we give voice to here. It is a reaction against the dominant rhetoric of 'tools', 'techniques' and 'frameworks' that give scant regard to the tacit abilities of the skilled practitioner and how we develop those skills. For example, we pay attention to the abilities in becoming attuned to relationships, contexts and the potential we see in others whilst having a humility that prevents us from jumping to conclusions and closing down possibilities.

One of the founders of OD, Edgar Schein, working in the 1960s, identified three basic modes in which OD people can work. He talked about the 'expert' role, the 'pair-of-hands' role and the 'collaborative' role. This advice is still useful today because it provides:

- A context in which the practitioner can ask themselves how best they can add value to the client.
- Linked to this, initial thoughts on the scope and the nature of any engagement from which expectations, desired outcomes and roles and responsibilities can be developed with the client.

In the expert role, we act like traditional consultants, observing the challenges of the system we are commissioned by, and making a diagnosis based on our expertise. In the pair of hands role, the OD person is more operational, acting on the diagnosis the client has already made about their own system. It is the collaborative role, sometimes also called the 'process role' that affords the OD practitioner a significant difference, and value, because it works in a way that suggests a more emergent, dialogue-based relationship between them and the client. In the words of Peter Block, who took Schein's ideas forward, in the collaborative role:

> Problem solving becomes a joint undertaking, with equal attention to both the technical issues and the human interactions involved in dealing with the technical issues.

> (Block, 2011, p.25)

This model of working, defined by the three roles, is a founding pillar of current OD thinking and practitioner training. At the core of it is an essential diagnosis of a problem in the client system. The value of the consultant is defined in terms of who has the authority to own this value-adding diagnosis – is it the consultant (the expert, like a doctor in her surgery), the client (where the consultant comes along and offers a 'pair of hands' to a pre-ordained set of outcomes) or is the diagnosis held dialogically between the client and their trusted OD 'process' consultant? On the surface, this looks straight forward particularly when compared with what happens in practice; here we bridge the gap by paying attention to a number of assumptions.

Emotional labour

One of the implications to which it is important to pay attention is the emotional labour of the consultant. The process/collaborative role inherently suggests that the OD consultant uses their own relational and emotional material, awareness and indeed life, at the service of the consultant–client relationship. This might be a good thing and indeed, OD is an area of practice that you could argue helps the practitioner develop and hone their emotional life. But it is important to consider the implications: unless we are careful, our emotional dynamic could become a commodity at the service of the organi-sation. This matters, because our emotional lives matter. Should our life become a commodity to be spent in service to an organisation? Arlie Hochschild, in her work, *The Managed Heart*, cautions us against the colonisation of private capacities for public use.

> What is new in our time is an increasingly prevalent *instrumental stance* [her emphasis] towards our native capacity to play, wittingly and actively, upon a range of feelings for a private purpose and the way in which that stance is engineered and administered by large corporations.

> (Hochschild, 2003, p.25)

Consider this recent example: an OD consultant was working internally in a large government department, at a very senior level. She worked very carefully and skilfully with the emotional process of a team of senior directors. The aim was to get them to come together when it looked like they were about to fragment in a way that would seriously affect the department. This took a high degree of emotional as well as technical expertise and was a great example of a process consultant doing their best work. After this had unfolded, the consultant was told by her boss, who was one of these senior directors, that he received a note from a colleague "thanking him for setting up a process so skilfully and carefully that enabled them all to meet their needs". She was understandably furious saying:

> He had done nothing! I had done all the work, both logistically and emotionally... I was exhausted at the end of it, and he was the one who got thanked.

This is an often-heard lament suggesting the longer-term fatigue, burn out and distress (emotional and even physical) that internal change people can experience. This isn't to say that we shouldn't do this work. It can be hugely emotionally rewarding. But it raises questions of the emotional labour we undertake. It suggests that we consider a subtle adjustment to how we configure ourselves, especially in times when the pressures and expectations are only increasing.

Craft

The problem with seeing ourselves merely as consultants is that it commoditises our emotional engagement with our work, with potentially serious implications. We suggest that this relationship can usefully be developed by seeing the nature of the deal with our practice as reciprocal, in a way that is more than just about financial or emotional reward. It could be about building ourselves as much as building the organisation. This brings in the notion of a craft at the centre of our practice.

The benefit of an OD practice-as-craft mindset is that it rebalances our sense of 'who benefits?' How could there be more of an ongoing intent to build ourselves, as an active component of our practice? Reconfiguring our practice as craft enables this. When a craftsperson does their work, there is an active social and emotional building of self as well as an external expression of creativity occurring. They are building themselves as well as building what they are crafting. In his book *The Craftsman*, Richard Sennett defined these inner and outer moves as being inextricably linked:

> This is *experience*, a fuzzier word in English than in German, which divides it in two, *Erlebnis* and *Erfahrung*. The first names an event or relationship

that makes an inner emotional impress, the second an event, action, or relationship that turns outward and requires skill rather than sensitivity. Pragmatist thought has insisted that these two meanings should not be divided. If you remain in the domain of Erfahrung, William James believed, you may be trapped by means-and-ends thinking and acting; you may succumb to the vice of instrumentalism. You need constantly the inner monitor of Erlebnis, of 'how it feels'.

(Sennett, 2008, p.288)

We need to hold on to our own sense of creativity, connection and relationship, for ourselves, in the service of our work. And therefore, we must not allow the involvement of our emotional lives in our work, important as this may be for our practice, to become merely an instrument in the service of the organisation. Thus we may avoid the burn out and fatigue that many change practitioners experience, as if their very soul has been poured down a bottomless drain of complex organisational dynamics.

So our practice is best seen as craft in which we both meet the needs of the system and maintain an active sense of what we are aiming to build in and for ourselves (see Figure 5.1). If we combine this with the main work of OD process consultants, which is sensitivity to the relationships around them, then you have an emerging picture of how an OD person starts to define their own strategy in their work, as a meeting point of:
- The relational life of the system, its human dynamics and politics
- The technical, on-the-ground, current business needs of the system
- The active and developing craft of the practitioner.

Figure 5.1: The development of one's craft within the organisational dynamic

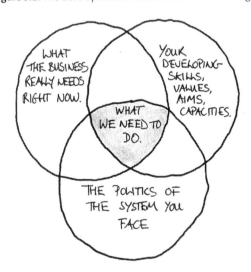

To be clear, this paradoxical inter-relationship is important for both the practitioner and the organisation. It puts some meaningful life back into the relationship, both internally and externally for the client and the consultant. Cheung-Judge and Holbeche talk about building a "self-care package" as part of developing our own capacity in our OD work: "Use self-knowledge to build a package of self-care... in order to ensure that instrumentality is sustainable and lasting" (Cheung-Judge and Holbeche, 2015, p.236).

What we are saying here takes this a little further: at the core of our craft of practice is a building of self that needs to be part of the deal; it is woven into the fabric. In fact, it could be argued that it helps to define the deal. The way you practise is contained to some extent in an inquiry about who you are and how you are living and developing your life. Your own story, mind, body, self, soul and spirit matter. They are core to this craft. It is about your life and the life of the system.

More than tools and techniques

Our practice is more that tools and techniques; it is also about the craft and the person, as James explains:

> A supervisor of mine, Denis Postle, used to talk about the need for those who work in any form of what he called 'psychopractice' (that is, the use of self in the practice of the work, be it therapy, counselling, coaching, OD or change practice at the human process level) to have regular, in-depth supervision of their work, in order for it to remain creatively engaged, actively connected with what Sennett called 'erlebnis' (Sennett, 2008). Postle talked about the need for our work as psychopractitioners to be 'baked afresh': as opposed to conducting some kind of received and ritualistic procedure, going through the motions, the work must have a quality of genuine connection and newness to it. This has implications for:
>
> - Supervision
>   (How are you being actively questioned, supported and challenged about keeping your own edge sharp?)
> - Developing and accrediting practice
>   (What is the best way of ensuring your craft is maintained and given some form of stamp of credibility?)
> - The long-term viability of being in OD
>   (How do you stay fresh and engaged?)

These and other practices are evoked in the light of noticing how often it is possible for one's colours to dim in the face of repeated human dynamics and organisational patterns. It can be very wearing and this can start to show in our practice. James goes on to explain:

Years ago, I was responsible for a personal development programme that ran for many years in a number of big organisations. It was a huge privilege and honour to run it, but after a while, I started to feel a bit numb to the repeating patterns I witnessed. Once, an experienced OD practitioner was amongst the participants. Afterwards, I asked him for some feedback.

"The programme is fantastic," he said. "People are getting loads out of it."

He paused.

"Go on," I said. "You look like you have got something else to say."

"Well, it is as if you have done this so many times that part of you is on autopilot. Don't get me wrong. I don't think it shows and the programme was great, but I just get that sense."

I was quite stung by this, but then hugely grateful. He was right. Part of me, some small creative centre, had gone to sleep, even without my realising it. It was one of a few prompts that suggested it was time to move on, not because I was doing a bad job or there was anything wrong with the programme, but in some way, I wasn't getting enough life, enough 'erlebnis', out of it. I had started, I think, to do what I have noticed a number of learning and OD people do: they stop learning themselves. It is what a friend of mine, Martin Saville calls 'hiding in plain sight'. This is to look like we are learning when actually we are fooling ourselves. We've stopped being 'baked afresh' in our work. It suggests that the work of craft in OD requires us to be prepared to inspect our own inner life regularly and perhaps, from time to time, move on to the next village.

As mentioned in Chapter 4, Yuri Slezkine (Slezkine, 2004), Professor of History at UCLA, USA has a formulation for this. He defines humankind in terms of two basic archetypes, going back many centuries— the Apollonians and the Mercurians. The Apollonians are agriculturalist, fixed to a territory and the Mercurians are essential nomadic and need to move on regularly. They are less fixed to a place and more to a set of ideas, and often a craft. For example, they are the circus folk, the knife sharpeners and traders that blow in and out of the village. He explains:

> As professional cultivators of people [rather than the land] Mercurians use words, concepts, money, emotions, and other intangibles as tools of their trade (whatever their particular trade may be). They assign value to a much larger portion of the universe than do peasants or pastoralists, and they see value in many more pursuits. Their world is larger and more varied – because they cross conceptual and communal borders as a matter of course...

> (Slezkine, 2004, p.28)

In this sense, the craft of OD is a Mercurian discipline, which by definition needs the constant refreshment of new vistas.

James concludes:

> This is what I had forgotten, before this brave practitioner, whose name I don't even remember, popped up in front of me and rang a little bell, before moving on himself.

Tools: what do they say about us and our craft

James reflects on his time working in a boat yard:

> Once, years ago, I worked in a boat yard. I spent a bright winter there, watching the grinding and welding of iron throw sparks under the starry sky, reflections bouncing off the river under the glinting flight path of Heathrow, in Isleworth. The Christmas twinkle lasted from October to February, when I was fired. I wasn't a very good boat builder. I was the sort of carpenter who built two-legged tables because I got bored before the third leg was finished. And there isn't much call for two-legged tables. But at least I learnt what being a good boat builder was all about.
>
> Boat work is the most skilled kind of carpentry. In fact it is much more than just carpentry: a good boat builder must learn to design, weld, engineer as well as fix and join wood, whilst fettling with diesel engines and the like, all without the help of a spirit level or a plumb line, the tools he'd be glad to lend you any time (as the old boat-builder joke goes) because they are useless to him on the water. (In those days, there weren't any women boat builders around – I wonder if that's still true.)
>
> The boat yard was on an island in the middle of the river and when the tide was in, we had to catch a lift from a boatman to work. Occasionally, when I wasn't falling in the river (which is another story) it was my job to ferry the workers, as it was a simple job that even I couldn't mess up too much. As I rowed back and forth across the river, I had a unique perspective on the boat builders at work. It seemed to me that there were broadly two types; let's call them Dave and Pete.
>
> Dave was bright and keen. He was (like me) more a boat builder by choice, rather than having been born into it. As such, he was keen to show what a natural he was. He knew lots and would be glad to tell you how much he knew. He was particularly well equipped. He had a big tool box, with the widest range of equipment. "You have to be prepared", he might say, as he'd show off the latest addition to his proud armoury. Once I heard someone say, perhaps unkindly, "Oh yes, Dave – all the gear and no idea." This was harsh. Dave was competent.

And what did I know? After all, I was really rubbish! But occasionally he would struggle with the odd, complex job because he didn't quite know which tool to use.

Pete, on the other hand, would have struck you as rather unimpressive at first glance. He was a bit dishevelled. Occasionally he would arrive late and hung over at the dockside, and greet me with a sheepish grin. No-one ever scolded him though. He would probably be carrying a milk crate and in it would be about 20 tools, maximum. Possibly fewer. They were good-quality tools, sharp but not impressive. What was most striking was the way Pete worked, when he fell to the job at hand. Like a demon, he would seemingly be able to apply himself to the most complex of joins, where all the angles converged like a wood block puzzle. He would be able to use his few tools in a range of bewildering configurations, and was seemingly never as stumped by the job at hand as he was by the simple things in life, like getting up in the morning in time for work. I liked Pete. He was kind and avuncular, born to life on the river. I once watched him apply himself to a particular challenge, involving what boat builders called a 'spile' — measuring up and cutting in a piece of irregularly shaped wood to a particular location of seemingly impossible proportions. It went in, first time, with the most satisfying of thunks, requiring no glue or screws. It was a work of art. I have worked with very many clever people in my life but rarely have I worked with true geniuses. I would number Pete amongst them.

The point of the story is that the tools weren't the thing. The reason why the tools weren't the answer in the boat yard, and may also not be the answer for us in the world of OD, is that the situations we meet are always unique. This isn't to say that tools are useless; far from it. Pete's twenty or so tools were good ones. He was happy to use them in very flexible ways. But the most important tools, of course, were within Pete himself: his mind, eye and hands, his whole self.

James reflects on the implications of his boat-building story to his practice today:

A recent conversation with my colleague and friend resonated with this story and its applicability to OD. We were discussing a particular organisation's approach to OD. They had a methodology that they were very passionate about. This is fair enough; it was a good method of change. But it struck him that they could be a bit monomaniacal about it: "How applicable is it in every situation", he said, "and what if they encountered a situation where it didn't fit so well? Would they adapt the tool or would they adapt the situation, making the world fit their own outlook?" An example of my own accords with this.

On a recent OD capability-building programme, in an action-learning set meeting, one person reported that their own organisation had a problem with competing methodologies around change. On the one side, there was the continuous improvement group, with a particular incremental view of change, using a project-management mindset. "Find the immediate problem, fix it, move on", as they put it. On the other hand, there were the appreciative inquiry advocates, who had a worldview that jarred against the whole ethos of continuous improvement: "look askance at the problems, focus more on what works and do more of it." The OD job here, as we came to see it in our action-learning set discussion, was not to take sides but to find a ground-level commonality between these two groups.

This is essentially a 'Mercurian' task: rather than another set of tools, this required modelling a mindset of dialogue, extemporising what can be made to work in a local, timely way. It doesn't really matter if in theory these worldviews are incommensurate because, in practice, the people involved could be facilitated to work together. It is a bit like the way any carpenter would frown upon the idea of using a screwdriver like a chisel, in theory; but if they find themselves on the job, fitting something at an awkward angle, and the screwdriver is what is to hand, they might be able to find a wangle with a quality outcome.

OD know how is about what works on the ground, rather than in theory. That is because the context is always changing and any set method will always find it hard to keep up with the dynamics of the here and now. So, tools aren't necessarily the thing in OD. One's outlook and a skilful use of the self are more important. Not that we would avoid using a few good sharp OD tools but we wouldn't stay too attached to them. Keep them in a milk crate and focus on your skilful use of yourself in the local context in which you are standing.

We found ourselves at the National Stone Museum in Derbyshire (yes, there is one) where they had an impressive display of dry stone walling from all over the UK, which varied depending on the local geography, geology and the nature and needs of livestock. Dry stone wallers work with what is to hand, fashioning enclosures for very practical purposes, such as keeping their sheep in one place. From a distance and individually, these walls look similar. Only when seen close up and side by side with one another can we appreciate the craft that has been developed over generations from what was at hand: a striking metaphor (see Figure 5.2).

Figure 5.2: Dry stone walling in some of its many forms, varying according to geology and need

This is also an entrée into the ways in which we talk about how craft develops, often orally and with practice shared between the expert and novice.

We spend a lot of time teaching people OD. The idea is that people want to learn how to do change in a more every-day, people-focussed way. So, how might we go about it? The answer is learning on the job with gentle support and challenge, often using action learning. This is a journey that is about craft and has spanned thousands of years: in the gendered language of the time, it is the progression from apprentice, to journeyman, to craftsman; and so the cycle repeats. In OD, as in other crafts, there is an initial yearning for tools and techniques. As time goes on, and students develop more confidence and more willingness to trust that they are going to be provided with what they need by the system they are in, if they pay attention to it, their need for tools diminishes. By then, they tend to have one or two rather sharp ones, which they use flexibly. But the real art, as in dry walling, is in combining the materials at hand in a creative and purposeful way. In OD work, the materials at hand tend to be in the form of people and their relationships with one another, and their relationships with you, the practitioner. They tend to be in the form of simple human processes, such as listening, working to develop greater clarity between people, paying attention to the dynamics in front of us, taking a risk that makes you vulnerable, being curious and sharing 'not knowing' just as much as 'knowing'.

As James reflects on his own journey and comfort with uncertainty:

> For myself, I measure my sense of confidence by the weight of the bag I carry around. In less confident times, I carry more stuff with me: pens, the inevitable Blu Tack and Post-It notes, games, toys, clever kits,

sometimes boxes and boxes of stuff. It was almost as if I could entertain people into change. As time's gone by, I have progressively lightened the load. I still carry a few Post-Its with me and a marker pen or two.

So, in practice, what are some of these components from which we develop our craft with the challenge and support of the trusted companions around us?

Emergent, systemic, complexity-based theory of change

We experience change that is emergent and complex. We read organisations as organic, open systems, following 'rules' of non-linear change. There is also the politics of planning, the rhetoric of the future state; leaders need to look like they know where things are going and that they know how to steer towards a desired vision of the future. This is as much about who they are and how they embody this desired future as what they think and decide. We therefore hold to emergence and work with leaders to manage their anxiety and develop their instrumentality around leadership in a complex, dynamic and unstable scene.

Wider ways of knowing (especially embodied)

Such a strategy requires intelligence at several levels. Traditionally, conceptual, 'thinking' intelligence is emphasised. We see people who lead change as more than just their conceptual ability – we hold their emotional, intuitive, physically embodied (somatic) and even transpersonal / systemic capacities as vital when it comes to working with complexity.

Relentless focus on inquiry and taking action (action research)

A complex system requires persistent learning – because its situation and specific challenges are always unique and in flux. While that doesn't mean that expert knowledge is redundant, it has its limits and is best used when it adapts to the local, timely and specific context of things. 'Living Life as Inquiry', as Judi Marshall put it, enables us to develop our knowing as we take action. This is a key component of our action-research approach. It is efficient, as it means we can 'learn by doing', developing what we know while making a difference in the system at the same time.

'Doing' OD to learn about it (rather than just talking about it)

We think that in a complex, dynamic system taking 'time out' to learn isn't always the most efficient method. Our view is that most learning in organisations can be gained while doing the business of the organisation. This is akin to the 70:20:10 axiom of the Center for Creative Leadership – 70% of learning takes place by doing, 20% by being coached or mentored whilst doing, and only 10% through theoretical knowledge. Our learning interventions and programmes are structured around the idea that the organisation is always 'in the room', and that the practices that people need can be developed in the here and now, while serving the system in real time.

Rejecting helplessness and moving towards the difficult

Our experience is that in the face of complexity, people can become helpless, resigned to the idea that things are too difficult to change. We believe that it is vital for people to find ways to practise rejecting helplessness and embracing possibility. Often this can involve a move towards the difficult things (such as conversations, relationships and situations) in a spirit of 'embodied generosity' and with an intent to be helpful to all involved.

Considering how you show up (in whatever you do)

By rejecting helplessness and moving towards the difficult, we would suggest that people can implicitly invoke the principle that there is a connection between their own personal system and the wider system(s) in which they are working. It follows that the way people 'show up' matters. Learning to understand (and ultimately master) the patterns that make up their approach, presence and impact is a life-long practice for people. We hold that it is through this practice that we learn vital things about ourselves, our work in the service of change and some of the fundamental structures that lie behind most human systems.

Phenomenological ('here and now') experience and the 'use of self as an instrument'

The patterns through which we 'show up' can help us learn about what is sometimes called the 'use of self as instrument'. This is a way of diagnosing and helping to change the systems we are working with. In our encounters with organisations, teams and individuals, we can use our experience in the here and now to create change by helping others to make sense of what is happening in different ways. This can help people broaden their perspectives, avoid harmful games and make wiser choices.

Building capacity in the system to serve itself

By encouraging our clients to move on without us, we also invoke a spirit of abundance rather than one of dependence. Our experience is that the quality of what we do will improve if we are working towards no longer being needed. We see all clients as potential co-researchers and partners, with the capacity to be peers. In this way, we are working towards encouraging every system we encounter to have the resilience and flexibility to serve itself.

Working with the unpredictable

According to Dan Gardner, author of *Future Babble: How to Stop Worrying and Love the Unpredictable* (2012), there are three critical attributes of wise 'foxes' – those who are more successful at reading what may happen in the future than others. He contrasts foxes with hedgehogs, those who predict the future with one big, often very black-and-white idea, which is almost always wrong. The critical attributes of foxes, which hedgehogs don't have, are:

> *Aggregation*: Foxes get their information from a wide range of sources, rather than a narrow band of 'expertise'.
>
> *Metacognition*: Foxes can think about how they think – that is, they self-critically analyse their own thinking styles, spot their own biases and adjust their view accordingly.
>
> *Humility*: Foxes extend this self-critical quality into an awareness that, when it comes to predicting the future, the complexity and non-linear nature of change involving people mean any prediction is likely to be wrong, more often than not. And that's OK.

What is really striking about Dan Gardner's work is how he emphasises that the above qualities don't actually help these fox-like sages to be better at predicting the future. In fact, this is almost impossible, because the nature of change is such that small variations in conditions can escalate to cause huge variations in the future. He claims moreover that, unless there is some radical, unforeseen invention of science, it is always going to be unlikely that we will get much better at predicting what will happen next. He avoids saying 'never' because, of course, that would be a prediction!

What he does say is that these qualities of aggregation, metacognition and humility help us in life because they help us deal with the fact that there is so much uncertainty.

The famous case study we mentioned in Chapter 4 of Honda motorcycles illustrates this. In the late 1950s, they sold their little 50cc cub bikes in the American market almost by accident and in direct contradiction to the rules of strategy that business schools may preach. The project leader, Kihachiro Kawashima (who went on to be president of Honda in the US), was initially reluctant, but was humble enough to recognise the opportunity for what it was. What Kawashima showed was humility and meta-cognition, as well as openness to (aggregated) sources of unexpected information.

What this suggests is rather than businesses wasting their time trying to create instrumental strategies that predict exactly how things will emerge, what may be better is to have flexible contingencies, and to breed the capacity to aggregate, meta-cognate and be critically self-aware, as these qualities will help leaders make the best contingencies for what might happen. Predicting the future may not be possible, but it is possible to teach the skills that help us live, and thrive, with this uncertainty.

Crafting in practice – finding value

We started this particular sojourn into craft by considering Schein's formula for the role that we as OD people choose as we enter the system of our clients. In this configuration, we are one of three kinds of 'consultant' and the value we add is packaged according to the nature of the diagnosis, who owns it and how authority is established for the next steps in the programme of work. There is a question here about the value an OD person can add. Value is defined fundamentally in terms of action. What do we do to move the client system on? This question implies the value we add is through agency. But how far does it capture the wider, deeper aspects of experience, and how value might be added in other ways, for example, by not acting – by simply being there and witnessing?

A story comes to mind. James was working with a senior team, in a healthcare setting. The team was beleaguered by the pressures of work and was experiencing a torrid time. James reflects:

> When I met with the team's head, he was convinced they needed a strategy, to think their way out of the mire. I met with each member of the team in a one to one. It was clear to me that they were all good people, thrown into conflict with each other by impossibly complex challenges and squeezed resources. Any rational strategy was countered by the ongoing emergencies they faced. As soon as they planned, events blew the plan out of the water. My heart went out to them. I felt like they needed to clear the air. I was scared to suggest this because they might consider doing more relational work was a 'waste of time'.
>
> Yet, I mulled it over and reflected that, if we didn't do this and instead simply rushed straight into some shiny strategy, I wouldn't feel that I

had offered them anything of real value. So I agreed with the manager that we should spend some time allowing this group to let off some steam. He wasn't that comfortable with the idea but trusted me enough to give it a go. I invited them to sit in a circle and review together the last few months, paying attention to their feelings. The group of eight people sat for a long time in silence. I felt anxious to intervene, to give them something more to work with. The manager looked pale. But instead, I bit my lip, sat and waited. Someone spoke. "Well this is how the last few months have been for me... !" and they proceeded to bravely expound. Others listened and nodded. I did too. More contributions came. I sat on my hands, waited, did very little besides listen. The atmosphere in the room was palpable. But then, like a storm breaking, the air cleared. 'I feel heard' was the spirit of the summing up. Once everything had been put onto the table, they started to organise their thoughts around what was needed next. The strategy that emerged wasn't a comprehensive, 'fix everything' document, but a series of steps that were 'available and adjacent' and most importantly, because they had all had space to be listened to, collectively agreed. We returned to the room a further four times across six months, adopting the same approach, making sure everyone was heard, and then agreeing what the next steps were together. It wasn't rocket science but it was a strategy.

After the first meeting the manager said to me "we couldn't have done that without you." But what did I do? I listened. I witnessed. I thought things that later someone else said, as if reading my mind. In thinking them, did I, in some quantum-like way, help them form their words, entangled with their thinking across the silence of the circle? And where was diagnosis, in that typical OD sense? The only diagnosis I had made or shared with them was my compassionate sense that they just needed a bit of time and some good-quality dialogue. In fact, was the quality of the dialogue improved by my not offering anything more complex? So, was I any type of consultant here? And how was the value of what I did quantifiable, apart from being there, acknowledging my own emotional response and perhaps role modelling a spirit of genuineness?

And to return to the boat yard...

When we refer to the 'tools and techniques' of OD, I imagine my friend Pete in the boat yard. A screwdriver or chisel in his hands was not the same tool it would have been in mine. In his case, the craftsman brought the tool to life – in mine, it was no more than a lump of metal.

So, to summarise, it may be that as the context of organisations becomes more complex and dynamic, and as more and more is expected of the OD practitioner (in terms of giving of their whole self, mind, body and spirit), there needs to be some kind of exchange in the commission that also allows for their development of self. In the same way that the craftsman, in Sennett's terms, requires both an inner and outer direction to their creative endeavour, so too does the OD practitioner.

The questions this chapter invites

- Given the pace and nature of change now, is there such a thing as a strategy for the organisation?
- If so, how long will it stay relevant?
- Is our capacity to predict the possible future in which content planning can take place enhanced by current technology or further diminished by the complexity it engenders?
- Do business schools have any relevance anymore and, if so, what type of know-how do they offer leaders?

Perhaps people in organisations still need strategies. Their purpose, however, in the light of the complexity we have discussed, may not be primarily to provide everyone with a complete and rigid set of steps into the future, but rather to help people engage in the first few steps, together, in an atmosphere of trust. In this way, when those first steps are taken and life intervenes to throw its inevitable curve balls, the relationships will be strong enough to adapt in a coordinated fashion. It is likely in future that we may develop a faith in technology that will give us a false sense of control. This may prove disastrous. Our role in OD in the next few years may be to defend emergence and speak up for human-scale change, in the face of increasing technological and social control. All too often, leaders think that the development of a strategy serves to create perfect clarity, when really what it does is help people trust each other better with uncertainty.

Photo: © Steve Marshall, www.drstevemarshall.com, @drstevemarshall

Politics and ethics of OD

Introduction

I N THIS CHAPTER, we explore the ethics of organisational development, a path not often trodden – at least explicitly. Doing the right thing is important for the OD practitioner's reputation and that of the client, particularly in the long term. There is the wider agenda too, one that Kurt Lewin would have appreciated – what is our role in creating a better world of work and a better world in general? This is particularly poignant at a time when technology is presenting humanity with unprecedented ethical challenges. Indeed, in our context here, these are already affecting organisational life. However, it can be challenging: sometimes the right things seem unclear or hidden. Group norms can sometimes push us down an avenue that we feel uncomfortable with, but the pressure seems too much to speak up.

There are times when groups are blind to what they are doing, having formed a way of working that is efficient in the short term but harmful in the long term. This will be explored more fully later but it is enough to say that ethical dilemmas can be hard to spot and harder to challenge. We are therefore cautious of any implication of 'I am ethical, you are not'; we are all part of the events that unfold. We are all interacting with each other and ethical dilemmas, albeit often small ones, present themselves frequently. In this chapter, we draw on a wide range of examples that brings this subject to life from several angles.

We will consider the topic from two connected perspectives:
- Designing in ethics before work starts
- Acting ethically in the moment.

These pose very different challenges: the former how we come to plan what we do and the latter how we act in the moment.

First, we will address how ethics tends to be treated in the OD literature and to see where there are some opportunities for exploration. Let us look at a respected book on the subject published by the Chartered Institute of Personnel and Development (CIPD), one of the professional bodies that includes OD. The book we have in mind is *People and Organisational Development: A New Agenda for Organisational Effectiveness* by Helen Francis, Linda Holbeche and Martin Reddington. The index has two mentions of ethics, one pointing us to CSR and the other to a couple of paragraphs split over two pages (Francis et al., 2012, pp.168–9). The section starts with an apology that a more in-depth discussion is beyond their scope. But what is said is relevant. It starts: "One of the main objectives of [critical HRD] is to reinstate ethics 'as a category of [organisational life]' through an attempt to preserve a harmony between the organisation's moral norms and the values and principles of social justice and equity prevailing in the wider operating context".

Whilst we recognise the importance of 'harmony', in our experience acting ethically occasionally means ruffling feathers, particularly if we are to change the way people, and we ourselves, relate to others. They go on to explain that critical HRD (an OD as a subsection of this) is a "guardian of workplace ethics" with the responsibility to resist the unfair treatment of employees. This seems a big ask on several counts. Firstly, where does this leave the responsibility of others, particularly in senior line-management functions? Could this attitude lead to an 'it's OK as long as we don't get caught' culture? Those in HR will not be expert in the culture, norms and practices of what goes on everywhere within the organisation and with stakeholders. Making anyone the guardian of something that they do not have oversight of is surely dangerous, as the banking crisis of 2007–8 showed.

Secondly, we notice that this book and others on the subject show a tendency to talk about organisations as if they were a reified physical entities, rather than of people who are working together on some joint organising enterprise. We pick this theme up elsewhere but there are implications for how people make individual choices, how these choices come to affect wider patterns of behaviour in the organisation and how individuals, affected by those patterns (often going back years in what we call 'culture'), make further choices. It sounds a bit deterministic, but we also see ourselves as individuals with some agency, able to make choices, albeit choices affected and influenced by those around us. Sometimes we are conscious of this but often not, particularly when we are embroiled in a culture and go with the flow.

What are the implications for us, as individuals, not in terms of grand descriptions of what it is to act ethically, but in those everyday ethical decisions we take in what we might call micro-ethical dilemmas? Our everyday interaction and experience is not with an organisation; it is with people in what we call an 'organisation'. We do not face abstract concepts, instead we relate to people and how we imagine they relate to us. It is in our imagination, developed through years of experience and intuition blended with the realities that we encounter, that we make choices that seem reasonable at the time. It is in this context (and mess) that we explore ethics.

The importance of addressing ethics explicitly

What we do can affect many people, many of whom we will never meet or even know of. When we facilitate an executive-level workshop, the result may be a large investment in a plant or its closure. In designing that workshop with the CEO, questions as to how the workshop will run and who will be there are part of a challenging conversation. Faced with a person with power and a different view, how are we to act? How hard do we push, particularly if we have strong reasons to believe the wrong course has been chosen? Sometimes these interactions can be rapid, a conversation in a corridor or a quick call, decisions in the space of a couple of minutes. What time do we have to reflect and consider the implications?

Set against this it can be easy to say "I act ethically in all my assignments"; but without carefully explaining to ourselves and others what this means and the dilemmas that we face, can we really say this? In addressing ethics explicitly, we seek to unravel these dilemmas and show the work to be done in making reasonable choices. By 'reasonable' we mean choices made with the best knowledge that we have to hand. This might be incomplete and contradictory, and the likely outcome may lead to something that is less than satisfactory. In doing this for ourselves, we can encourage this thinking in others and thus have a greater impact. The effects of our involvement will have ripples and often amplify throughout an organisation and beyond. We have a responsibility to take in what we do and what we cannot.

Designing in ethics before work starts

Both of us supervise students' postgraduate research projects as well carrying out our own research. We are going to use the example of ethics approval in research because it is an explicit form of a practice that is often implied in organisational development. This will enable us to explore the problems and opportunities of an approach to ethics that seeks to 'design in' safeguards at the start but sometimes pays little attention to the issue thereafter.

In the world of research, ethics approval must be obtained before any data collection can occur, which requires a signed form that will often be discussed at a committee. The objective is to ensure that no-one comes to harm (the people involved in the research activity, the researchers, the organisation, the university and so on) and that the potential knowledge outweighs the time and effort of everyone's involvement – all very reasonable. In filling it in, the researchers have to answer questions about their research objectives, their methodology and what they hope to achieve. This is not wasted effort as the outputs are often to be used in their final write-up but, more importantly, it challenges them to think and to work through a number of scenarios, to make improvements and to make the project better and safer. Occasionally, there is a challenge and their methods have to be changed, their work re-drafted or even refused.

In a less rigorous way, similar processes happen in agreeing an OD assignment, although more often than not these stages are implied. What are the assumptions in this approach and what might they obscure? There is an assumption that knowledge and ethics conform to a scientific paradigm, namely of the linear process from theory, through hypothesis, data collection, findings, confirmation or otherwise of hypothesis, to the revision of the original theory and so on. This is a form of ethics that is well-suited to testing the behaviour of mice in Skinner's box, where we are in control of the variables and there is a neat separation between subject and object, namely of ourselves as experimenters and those under investigation.

This problem was brought home vividly for Rob when working with a student who was keen to use ethnography. Ethnography (Ellis and Bochner, 1996) is a form of research whereby one works with people during their normal day-to-day activities. It is the study of the mundane, the very normal activities that form the practice of our everyday lives that would otherwise go unnoticed. Fitting a very naturalistic methodology into a linear research ethics format was awkward for the student. Although this approach to ethics is helpful in imagining what might happen and to design a safe and ethical method, it can only go so far. One can only explore broad themes that might arise and how those can be dealt with. But we know unplanned events occur, some of which are surprising, to which we have to react (or not) and for which we may well have to justify our actions later on. The actions that we take, even a quick conversation in a corridor, can have consequences for many. It is also likely that the interesting insights that are at the heart of this approach will arise from these unplanned and emergent encounters. But of course, these won't have featured on our ethics form.

Moving our gaze from the research agenda towards organisational practice, the scientific method, with its roots in the enlightenment and the work of Emanuel Kant, still looms large. Take for example the work done in drafting a strategy. Workshops are held, different perspectives are sought, communities of stakeholders are engaged with and then a view of the future is formed and this is articulated in a strategy. Often this might include a description of the external factors, capabilities and capacities within the organisation, new opportunities and threats to consider and a series of actions to embark upon. Each strategy comes with a view as to what the future will look like. Sometimes these are articulated in broad statements but often as targets to be achieved along with numbers (an increase in profits, units sold, geographies expanded into and so on). We therefore have a view of the future, there is an assessment of what needs to be done and these are agreed along with targets to be achieved. Roll forward a few months, a year, and the busy manager is caught between two stalls. On the one hand, *the past* – her activities have already been mapped in the strategy written some time ago; and on the other, *the future* – she is beholden to future expectations in the form of those targets. Ralph Stacey, a complexity theorist of how people relate to each other, refers to this as a 'formative teleology'. Following a Kantian tradition, the future has already been defined and what is required is an unfolding process to make this evident (Stacey, 2001). What is lost is the attention paid to the present, the dilemmas and opportunities that manifest themselves in the here and now. Instead of a formative teleology, Stacey refers to a transformative teleology as being a perhaps more significant feature of organisational life. This way of thinking pays attention to the movement towards an unknown future that is under perpetual construction by the interaction of people as they progress together. This human endeavour is fundamentally paradoxical: it both sustains continuity but at the same time creates novelty into an unknown.

This movement holds the potential for transformation, but there is no optimal condition or fixed plan that is to be revealed. In this sense our future is both unknowable and recognisable (Stacey, 2001, p.163). Rather than being under the shadow of Kant, Stacey is influenced Hegel and the nature of process. This is not to say that thinking of ethics as a plan is without merit, but it is limited and needs to be seen in context and in relation to ethics in action. Philip Hancock talks about a quality of 'embodied generosity' as a bridge between the Kantian and complexity worldviews. The idea of embodied generosity asks us to consider our intent as we embark on any piece of research or OD work. It suggests that although we can't necessarily plan for what might happen, we shouldn't abdicate our responsibility, throw up our hands as if to say "Well, nothing is knowable about what might happen so my ethical position is one of abdication"; rather our intent should be to 'do right' by all players. In so doing we should embody an invitation of trust and responsibility, in that we will do our best to follow through with any ethical considerations that may emerge.

> What I hope I have suggested here, is that if this is to be achieved it will
> not be through compliance [i.e. Kantian] or the actions of isolated
> subjectivities [i.e. postmodern], but rather through the emergence of a
> mutual recognition of, and state of generosity towards the other; one

that seeks not closure but a genuine openness to difference, creativity and the conviviality of an ethical organizational life.

(Hancock, 2008, p.1,371)

Hancock's position asks us to pay attention to how invested we are in any human system we enter, as researcher or OD consultant. We do so as passionate players, rather than dispassionate observers.

So a research ethics form (or its implicit equivalent in a piece of OD work) is an exercise of social imagination. It gets people together to talk through what might happen for good and ill, what we might like to pay attention to and what actions we might take to help us on our course. However, this is limited and should be seen as such. In light of this, what are the ways of noticing and behaving ethically in the unfolding situations that we face on a day-to-day basis? It is this that we pay attention to in the next part of this chapter. However, we do so not to negate the importance of ethics as we have described it so far.

Acting ethically in the moment

If in the *past* we have written a strategy and in the *future* we become beholden to its tasks and targets, the actual *present* may feel reduced to a dot in time in which we have little agency, we are hemmed in. This is the risk of a strategy, or OD agreement, in which there is no room to move, interpret or react to events and opportunities. That is a risk, for there are dilemmas to be dealt with and hard work to be done.

To start the process of exploring the present, we turn to George Herbert Mead, an early US philosopher of the pragmatist school. Within the chapter 'The Present as the Locus of Reality' (Mead, 1932), in a collection of works called *The Philosophy of the Present*, Mead pointed out that our past is subject to reinterpretation in the light of our knowledge of what we are facing today. And in this interpretation, emergent possibilities become apparent to us. In this sense, the re-imagining of our past with our present enables us to imagine and make decisions for the future. And yet paradoxically, the quality of the past is never entirely lost to us (Mead, 1932, p.37).

What does this mean with respect to one's experience of the present and of acting ethically? In making sense of our current situation, we draw on past experiences, either consciously or as a reflex-like action. As we react and experience reaction, we reinterpret our pasts. All of this is in the context of the decisions we take to move forward into a future that is unpredictable yet with characteristics we can rely upon. We expect it to be different, but not completely so. The present is thought of as a dot in time, that unravels to influence, and is influenced by, the interpretations of the past and sensing of the future. It is for these reasons that we spend the majority of this chapter addressing the ethics of the 'living present', the everyday experiences that occupy our thoughts and actions. It is noticeable that one of the earliest and most famous experiments in OD, Lewin's T-Group of 1946, could be thought of as a laboratory of the living present. The following is a short narrative of being caught between the past and future in which a practitioner is trying to make sense of what is happening. Rob explains:

> In this situation, the issue of targets was contentious and had become an issue of commitment amongst the board. So, although the figures within the targets were known to be based upon weak information and were unreliable, the targets were still very important. Several months after the strategy was agreed, a colleague and I sat down, as we regularly did, to review what had happened (i.e. performance) against the targets. The focus of our conversations was not what was happening and what had happened and how we were making sense of it. The conversation was directed instead at why there was variance with the target in the strategy, a target we knew to be largely arbitrary. For example, we had committed to transfer over four teams to a new employer; however, due to technical reasons... this was unlikely for one team. Instead of sticking with three and doing them well, we 'evoked the contingency plan' to start bringing another team over.

This narrative highlights an ethical decision of how and when to act during the course of a meeting – or whether to act at all. Note the sense of dilemma and tension. James explores this further with another example:

> Some time ago, I was at a meeting of a governance board of a public-sector body. The organisation had proposed an investment of several million into new services. Up until this meeting we only had verbal updates as to how things were progressing. It was a complex and expensive project for the organisation. Yet the thirty or so people on the board did not raise any concerns. Questions for me, over and above cost and the nature of the new service, included the impact on the culture of the organisation, how it might divert our attention from what we were already doing, the impact on the local community and so on. Now, it was not that these conversations were not happening; they were, but not here – a major governance committee of this organisation.
>
> The ethical dilemma for me was whether to raise an objection or concern in the meeting, or keep quiet and go with the flow. Doing what I thought was right came with personal reputational risk. But I spoke with my boss beforehand and he was supportive and shared similar views. This gave me confidence, but I knew he would not be there. The time came. The verbal report was given and there was some conversation about the project. I addressed the chair and raised my

concern. At this point I sensed a few antibodies were released and defensive remarks were made by a couple of people heavily involved in the project. I and the rest of the meeting were "assured" that procedures were followed and that everything was in order. I felt awkward, slightly panicky and a little flushed, and I was losing my knack of putting words together, but I carried on. It was not that these procedures were not being undertaken, but that there was a lack of appropriate visibility – in other words, assurance. I had worked on projects before where this had been a problem. In fact, I lecture in this subject. I carried on with my point, sensing more antibodies, then I stopped. The chair said that they would look into it and report back at the next meeting. I felt that I had made a mistake, albeit I felt that I had made the right decision.

Two days later my boss called me into his room. He showed me the screen of his computer, which was displaying an email trail that the events of the board meeting had sparked. I had created ripples that I had been unaware of. There was a flurry of comments from the senior leadership team taking my comments on board and working out what they were going to do. A few days later, I had coffee with a colleague in another department who knew someone at the meeting and commented on my intervention and gave me an overview of other ripples of impact that I was also unaware of.

There is nothing unusual about this story; it is likely that you have had a similar experience. And that is the point: over the course of the average week, many such dilemmas are faced in organisations and amongst their people. These might be personal needs, their team, organisation or a mixture, with motivations of altruism or selfishness. However, they will rub up against each other. This will occur socially between people even when they are 'singing from the same hymn sheet'. It will even occur within the contradictory thoughts, feelings and actions of one person. In addition, this plays out in the interaction between us in groups and us as individuals.

Thought of in this way, OD spans the big set pieces of the 'town hall meeting', running a workshop or long-term piece of cross-organisational re design, to an informal conversation with an aspiring director over coffee that results in her being able to interpret what has happened in a fraught meeting. In these contexts, ethical challenges emerge.

The big ones are easy to spot and are often straightforward; the small one less so, both in terms of how we might notice them and how to deal with them. We call these 'micro-ethical dilemmas'.

Micro-ethical dilemmas – the daily challenges

We start this section by exploring some events that were going on behind the scenes of Rob's narrative, discussed in the previous chapter (see pages 75 to 77), about designing a workshop and how events unfolded.

> I was part of a group working on a major restructure. It involved a hundred or so nurses changing employer. This process, part of a larger change initiative, required new roles and job descriptions. A team had been working on this and had drafted new job descriptions ahead of a couple of large consultation workshops with the staff that I was facilitating. Two questions came up: should we send the job description to them before hand or give them out on the day? And should we add a few mistakes to make them appear as if we had rushed them? I felt queasy on both counts and whilst the second was rejected, we stuck with the idea of handing them out on the day so we might not have quite so many challenging questions. In facilitating the workshop, I felt the tension in the room as the documents were handed out, it felt like exam day at school. People expressed frustration that they were not given out earlier, but soon quietly settled down to reading them. As well as the nurses there were also directors and senior managers of the services sitting separately on tables that looked slightly more important. Their explanations at the start were confident and assured. After the documents had been read though, their confidence slipped as they faced grounded technical and personal questions about how the service would run and issues of pay and shift working.

Was it ethical to withhold information until the last minute? Was it ethical to create an impression? You can sense that these issues were discussed. Although the word 'ethics' was not used, we did ask "is this the right thing?" This was a big change programme and there was little experience for the team to draw on. We were nervous and keen that it went well. The decision to withhold the documents had an impact on the day, as we saw in the last chapter: it affected the nature of the conversation, beginning with irritation in the group. Although the participants were disoriented by this, they quickly gathered their thoughts and started to ask very contextual and demanding questions. As the discomfort of the directors and senior managers grew, they became more confident and sure footed. The project was a success; questions were eventually addressed. The ethical decision had an impact, and this was reacted to and the conversation moved on; here it was a blip, but this is not always the case. Sometimes these everyday decisions have greater impact down the line. They are processes that evolve over time and can amplify. But there can also be important contradictions that add to the ethical problem.

On the one hand, an ethical dilemma can become greater; but on the other, it can also become harder to recognise – and if recognised, it can become difficult to resolve. By this we mean a person can become drawn into the social melee in which their ability to speak and to hold to account reduces. This is for a number of reasons, some of which are explored below.

Being drawn in – the small gift. In this situation a small gift is made for which you feel an obligation. Sometime later, the giver asks a favour, very small and innocuous, and you feel obliged. Another gift is made and friendships are forming and another favour is asked. You form an effective working relationship with this individual but also with their networks. And this is how it continues. But then a favour is asked about some information that is on the cusp of what you think is acceptable, but you provide it. In this act, you have now become dependent on them and they have a stake in you. A bolder request is made and the mutual obligation is drawn attention to and again you relent. This time, the request is more serious and compromising: you are caught.

In this situation the ethical dilemma only becomes apparent when it is too late, there is little chance of going back and the only course of action is to withdraw (leave the organisation) or to own up as to what has happened. This latter option has its challenges: the relationship that you are now part of only has its strength in those networks of mutually assured destructive trust; each is beholden to the other. The network tightens and becomes defensive: what is your choice now?

A lone voice – the draw of collusion. You join a team that has been working together for several years. Its members see the world in a very similar way to one another and, when faced with challenging news, back each other up to establish a more comforting view of reality. Despite what you see as being common sense, they disregard your views and back each other up with greater energy. You try to take a halfway position on another issue using language which they relate to and toning down the message. This gets a better reaction but is still rejected. You accommodate further and in doing so you find acceptance. You feel you're having an impact with nods around the table but limited future commitment. Months later you reflect: what has changed? In fact, nothing has, apart from you.

On the first day working in a new organisation, everything seems vivid; within a week what was vivid is now dull. The same goes for relationships. In this example, we see the process of compromise that was necessary for getting one's voice heard, but also how it comes to affect our view. The question is: how would the first day 'you' react to what you have become? The balance between your accommodation of language and understanding of how things work needs to be matched against the change your words and actions are having. If that balance does not shift, one has to ask: what is the correct next step?

The long-term coach – morphing into one. Some years ago you were approached to coach an aspiring director. You got on immediately with each other, making a strong connection both culturally and in your view of work and relationships. She is now one of your only clients and you genuinely like her. She has become a senior director of a large organisation and as you enter the room, you notice that you are wearing similar clothes. The pattern of conversations repeats itself; the same people are talked about in similar ways. The challenge that you put in serves to reinforce known values and views that you know she has; there is now little surprise in any conversation you have with her. You're talking to a mutual acquaintance one day who reflects on how similar you both are and asks the question: who does this relationship benefit? You realise there is a mutual dependency.

You realise this may not serve your client: she is not being challenged to see her world from a different angle. Instead you are now only serving to reinforce decisions that have been quickly taken and are now starting to unravel. Is it better to go your separate ways?

Anticipating the boss – action before it is asked. There is a Japanese word, *sontaku*, meaning to anticipate one's boss's next wish and to take action accordingly (Lewis, 2017). The boss may never know what you have done. On the one hand, this might be efficient; but it allows the boss deniability. It is governance by anticipation with no evidence trail. Not only does the term relate to action taken, but also to actions not taken, for example self-censorship. Not wanting to upset powerful people, decisions are taken by individuals not to ask awkward questions; or on a larger scale, a media corporation fails to investigate serious allegations. This is not new or confined to Japan: the musings of Henry II ("Who will rid me of that troublesome priest?") had consequences for Thomas à Becket. Similarly, in her controversial discussion of Adolf Eichmann's trial (Arendt, 1963), Hannah Arendt she observed that, although Eichmann was a gifted administrator and had developed an ability to anticipate his master's next wish, he was neither smart enough nor had the reflexive abilities to ask himself the question: "Is this right?" The consequences, as we all know, were dreadful. So, the implication for Japan today is economically and politically substantial. And as for Thomas à Becket, one can still visit the scene of his murder in Canterbury.

The examples here might seem extreme; but such situations exist more subtly in the tone and culture of organisations. You need a level of authority to adapt to changing situations in a way that recognises your understanding of a context that your boss does not possess. But at what point is there ethical over reach? And as a boss yourself, how do you justify knowing what is happening and allowing it to develop?

Spatial and temporal connections

A common theme in these cases is the issue of how interaction changes over time. Small decisions that seem harmless (or pass unnoticed, even) build up and affect how we react to others and how they react to us. As we become accustomed to a new client and they get to know us, the ability for us and those around us to notice and challenge diminishes. A part of this is essential as we enter new worlds, but it comes with risk. This risk includes damage to ourselves and those we work with. The dilemma of when to speak up is not straightforward particularly when one is becoming increasingly invested in that world. By investment, we mean not only commercially but reputationally and morally – and in extreme cases, legally.

Another theme is spatial: the number of people affected at any particular moment, spread over a team, organisation and/or sector. As John Donne said (in the gendered language of his day): "no man is an island". A decision, either to do or not do, has implications for the decision maker but also for others. Sometimes these people are known, but often not and the impact can have surprising ripple effects. So our actions can have wide effect as demonstrated in earlier narratives.

Both spatial and temporal play out together in ways that may be predictable and surprising, requiring deft skill and intuition to navigate what is often a highly political context. And the dangers and opportunities are dynamic. Take the start of a new project: when one is new to a situation, it can be hard to figure out what is going on, but then you may well be given leeway and that very naivety may serve you and your client well. Or it might not. Roll forward six months: you have settled in, what once seemed surprising is now routine and goes largely unnoticed. Your ability to challenge dims as does the acceptance of you challenging. Your ethical challenges are now different: for example, to develop your ability to notice and to have challenging conversations. Towards the end of your assignment, how you disengage from your client has ethical challenges too. For example, an ethical question might be: how do you develop a culture of learning in your client organisation so that it can address similar issues rather than developing a culture of dependency?

One final story – of politics and connections

To illustrate the impact we have with people and organisations here, we offer a conversation that a practitioner had with a senior person in an NHS trust. It demonstrates the political nature of OD, its randomness and how a brief conversation can have ripples for many. As the practitioner explains:

> I am brought in to meet a senior leader in a hospital to talk to them
> about their imminent retirement. As they explained:

"I have worked here for nearly 30 years. The last couple of years have been a bit of a grind. I am due to retire in November. The CEO asked me not to just go. She said, 'Tell me what you want to do. Write your own job spec, based on what you think we really need.' So the plan is, I will retire, and then come back and fill in where I can add most value. The problem is, I don't know where that is in the current system. I need some help to think that through."

So we explored this system, drawing the current constellation of roles and organisational challenges on a piece of paper. The set of scribbles and boxes, lines and arrows reminded me of Margaret Wheatley's depiction of the real organisational map (Wheatley, 1999), compared to the official organogram that is usually drawn.

The challenge she faced boiled down to a simple question, with a complex set of possible responses. We discussed what she would want as she stepped out of her current role and towards the next one. She wanted to:

- Have a clear mandate on behalf of the current Executive Director – we identified three possible options.
- Work directly with clinical departments, helping their leadership teams, or at least coaching these teams to do it for themselves.
- Fit in with (and avoid clashes with) current senior operational deputy directors.
- Do some enjoyable work on a part-time basis.

The first of these took up a lot of our time. It was a discussion about who would be the best fit, personality, skills and mandate-wise. In the end, she described our conversation as "surprisingly useful", which I took as a compliment. What struck me though was a rather chilling moment in relation to the role of the organisation's existing OD function in the scheme of things.

In the course of sketching out the map of relationships and roles, and exploring the consequences of this special, roving role that she sought, it occurred to me that what she was doing was effectively a piece of organisational design and development work. We were talking about relationships, strategy, culture and leadership, whilst trying to figure out the best design, in terms of the orientation of the pieces of the organisational jigsaw in front of us. At one point I mentioned this to her. Her response was to say: "Yes I am, but I can't call it that, because OD sits over here…" and she drew a tiny box, right at the edge of the piece of paper, reporting to one of the two central corporate divisions, which she had already ruled out as fairly unimportant in her thinking, in favour of the more central, clinical departments.

It struck me as ironic that here she was 'doing OD', yet the people tasked with doing OD in the system were regarded as right on the edge of the map. One saving grace of this, I suppose, is that my entry into the organisation was through this tiny, marginal (and in my opinion excellent and hard-working) OD unit. So in a sense, as their proxy, I was doing the 'real OD' for them, and on their behalf, by having this conversation. But it wasn't widely regarded as such.

What are we to make of this? This conversation had the potential to affect the lives of many people, but it would have been easy not to recognise this or its ethical obligations. There was no neutral or completely safe position: to act or not to act would have consequences. The individual was facing a real dilemma of not only what to do, but how to go about it. As the conversation was progressing, there were implications for those who were unknown, even the organisation's OD department. The 'right thing' was not easily identifiable – indeed there was no one right answer, only perhaps answers that were better than others in the context of being interpreted. During the course of a year, say, there will be many conversations and decisions exerting competing and complementary pressures on those involved and it is through this that change emerges. The choices we make have the potential for harm or good, or both.

The (de-)politicisation of OD

As an important subtext to the ethical questions we consider in this chapter, one final point we'd like to make is that OD was originally conceived from a strongly political standpoint. We wonder whether that standpoint has been lost, or at least diluted. It is important to remember that many people conceive of OD, including some of its founders, in terms of social liberation. Take Kurt Lewin, for example. As an escapee of Nazism in 1930s Germany, he was deeply committed to the possibility that the practice he was developing with colleagues could lead to more enlightened social relations, or at least forestall fascism's rise:

> These activities chimed with one of [Lewin's] central preoccupations, which was how Germany's authoritarian and racist culture could be replaced with one imbued with democratic values. He saw democracy, and the spread of democratic values throughout society, as the central bastion against authoritarianism and despotism.

> (Burnes, 2004, p.980)

The problem is that, as it has become mainstream, particularly in the business world, we could suggest that these deep values intrinsic to the thinking behind OD methods and approaches have been stripped away from the methods themselves. They have become fair game, available for any organisation to use, irrespective of either its own product and purpose, or the managerial intent behind it. Could a company with a purpose that many would regard as immoral use the instruments of OD to further itself, even if that meant oppressing people or poisoning the planet?

We don't suggest what the purpose of such a company might be – you can make up your own mind about that; but does the use of OD tools to this end suggest a debasing of our collective professional currency? Similarly, if we put aside the 'what' of the organisation to consider the 'how', many corporations with products of laudable social value might have a poisonous culture, for which the application of OD approaches may act as a kind of fig leaf. Professor Chris Grey of London University argues that ultimately the power of corporatism and its bureaucratic narrative is so strong that all sorts of laudable social innovations are imprisoned by it and turned to its purpose, which is efficiency and social control. OD is no exception in that regard. He discusses at length the discourse in management text books about two sorts of managers, one of whom is 'rational', emotionless, controlling and authoritarian and the other, called Val, who uses a more 'OD-ish' approach:

> Val takes a more human relations type of approach. She tries to understand the problems and anxieties of her staff and to encourage their wider motivations to work. But – and this is the crucial point – they both sought to control their teams: one by avoiding human relationships and one through human relationships.

> (Grey, 2009, p.47)

This is a vital point. If OD becomes a useful tool for manipulation, then it isn't OD at all, at least not in any sense that people like Lewin imagined it. Ultimately, though, Grey and others argue that the human worker isn't biddable. They catch on quickly and find subtle, clever ways of subverting the system anyway. James C. Scott calls these 'hidden transcripts', the 'in your face', irrefutable ways that people rebel without costing them their jobs (or even their lives) (Scott, 1990). We witness this in many guises, from water-cooler gossip circles and graffiti in toilet cubicles to simple non-compliance and even more creative subversions.

A case in point is that of a global steel-manufacturing company, whose chief executive had recently become enamoured of the work of the American OD guru, Jim Collins, and his well-known study of highly successful companies, *Good to Great* (Collins, 2001). He decided that all the senior managers of this company should read the book and it should become core to the company leadership strategy. This is something of an irony, because one of Collin's key messages is that change shouldn't be imposed from above; success should be gradual and unglamorous, achieved by carefully noting and incrementally building on what works. The senior-manager community at this steel company became highly adept at using all of the buzzwords in Collins's book, throwing around ditties about 'flywheels', 'hedgehogs 'and 'level five leadership' with glee. It was pure mickey taking, but in a carefully measured way so that the CEO couldn't really object. Meanwhile, none of *Good to Great* was taken seriously. So the moral of this story, we suggest, is that not only is it at some level unethical to impose OD instruments on communities at work in the hope that it forces compliance, but that people are clever enough to know, generally, what you are doing and good at undermining such artlessness. Indeed, Scott begins his book with the following Ethiopian proverb: "When the great lord passes, the wise peasant bows deeply and silently farts" (Scott, 1990).

Doing OD, as with most things, is an inherently political set of activities. Despite the pretence of objectivity inherent in the content and tone of traditional management literature, there is no such thing as apolitical work with people. As individuals, and indeed as a profession, we do our best to face our intentions, as we go about our work, always prepared to ask ourselves the famous question, "cui bono?" Who stands to benefit?

The questions this chapter invites

- How is the imperative of liberation and justice in the workplace still relevant?
- What is the work to be done in questioning the purpose of an organisation and how it goes about its activities?
- What are the micro-ethical dilemmas in your working relationship and what will you do?
- When we listen to the hidden transcripts, the gossip and corridor conversations, what are people angry, complacent or happy about now? And what should our reaction be?

The ethical challenges in OD increasingly mirror those in organisations more generally and our actions (and non-actions) can make this better or worse. There is no neutral position: even being present in a conversation and not saying anything has an impact. We can even do this without thinking about it or by stumbling into conversations where the impact is felt further in the future by many people.

On the one hand, planning an ethical approach at the beginning of any assignment is important but so too is paying attention to those everyday interactions that we might otherwise not think twice about. We can usefully adopt what Hancock calls 'embodied generosity', recognising that we are never neutral instead always maintaining, in principle, a commitment to the consequences of what we are involved in (Hancock, 2008). It may also be significant that some of the most compelling places of practice and development for OD practitioners may be in 'here and now' work, moving towards the ethical challenges and dilemmas with some skill and intent to work them through. It is in the 'nick of time', as the philosopher Elizabeth Grosz puts it, that significant change may happen, as it does in nature, according to natural selection (Grosz, 2004). Learning to seize the moment of opportunity may be one of the things an OD practitioner can best learn to do.

And then there are those micro-ethical dilemmas, those small ethical choices that can go unnoticed but whose impact can be substantial, affecting both the organisation and ourselves. The implications can grow over time, sometimes slowly; and spatially, these implications can be felt beyond our immediate interactions to people we do not know or know about. Our responsibility is substantial and honouring this takes reflexive thought and consideration of our actions and thoughts, both in planning and in the moment of our interactions with others.

Photo: © Steve Marshall, www.drstevemarshall.com, @drstevemarshall

7

The impact of what we do

Introduction

W E WILL BEGIN BY explaining what this chapter is not about. We do not address how one goes about measuring impact and the merits or otherwise of opting for quantitative analysis over qualitative; or the techniques one would use in carrying out a focus group or designing a questionnaire. There are many OD and management research books that cover these topics. But there is a problem with measurement if that is all one looks at. In his book, *Seeing Like a State*, the anthropologist James C. Scott illustrates this with the story of the arrival of settlers in North America. In trying to work out when to plant the new seeds they had obtained from their Native American neighbours, they were confused to be told to "plant corn when the oak leaves were the size of a squirrel's ear": they were hoping to be told a particular time of year. For the Native Americans, the calendar was governed by the contextual orderly succession of events and required the paying of close attention to the local weather, fauna and flora (Scott, 1998, pp.311–12). Whist the actual timing varied, the choice of when to plant was precise within this natural order. In this chapter, we will consider the holistic nature of measuring impact, particularly context.

We are addressing the question: what is it that we are doing when we talk about measuring impact? In other words, what is going on and what assumptions do we bring with us in the conversations we have with clients and others? There is thus an important step before evaluation: to understand what we value and why. And then there are the following linked questions: what are we paying attention to and what are we leaving in the shadows? As we have already discussed how we go about the ethical and political consequences of OD, this also extends to how we go about demonstrating impact.

There is another angle too: sometimes we do not like to recognise the good work that we do. It was the aim of Kurt Lewin, who did much to shape OD in the period after the Second World War, to improve the world of work. In holding onto that spirit we should not be ashamed to demonstrate to others and ourselves the positive impact we have – and in so doing, to continue Lewin's promise in this changing world.

What is going on when we talk about impact?

"Not everything that can be counted counts and not everything that counts can be counted."
(Often attributed to Albert Einstein and Oscar Wilde)

The conversation begins: "We need some tangible outcomes. We need to demonstrate some impact." It is an important question, even though it can be irritating and challenging. There are good and bad reasons for this irritation. A bad reason is that OD practitioners can be quite mercurial. They tend to move on to the next thing, mirroring the mercurial nature of the organisations they work alongside. We can therefore be our own worst enemies when it comes to our ability to tell longer term stories of the impact our work has had. It is also challenging because if we take the question seriously, we need to unravel what is meant by 'impact', its limitations and how we are all involved in the activity.

In this chapter, we raise questions in order to give OD people some confidence in speaking up for themselves. We also want to change the debate towards longer-term impact, particularly the heuristic processes by which we assess, learn and take action. The 'we' here being all of us – for example, us as OD practitioners, our clients and the teams and individuals we work with. But we appreciate that this is hard.

When we hear the question about impact, we also hear the anxiety of the client. Perhaps her career, or at least reputation, is on the line. It may well be the case that we need to be mindful of the conversations that she will be having with a sceptical boss or colleagues who might be asked to release staff to attend a course. But more fundamentally, we are starting the process of affecting the power dynamics that our client is embroiled in and this might well be frightening. Perhaps for us, these might be important clues as to how the engagement might go.

In the chapter 'The essential fluidity of OD and organising', we also described the problematic nature of how we measure OD activity in relation to how it comes to affect the entire organisation. We drew on the analogy of reading a book and how a word or sentence 'dissolves' in the meaning-making activity of the reader as they come to assimilate and understand the entire text in the context of their own experience. So to ascribe organisational or even depart-mental impact from a discreet number of activities is problematic.

We have therefore identified three challenges: the anxiety of our client with reputations to build; our own mercurial tendencies in OD to move to the next thing; and the problem in thinking that cause can be thought of in the same category as effect.

On occasions, we have both been surprised by the focused questions that demand certainty as to what the future will bring, particularly set against a backdrop of organisational uncertainty. When people talk about measures, tangible outcomes or quantification, it is worth pausing to understand the underlying motivations.

James reflects:

> I remember being involved with an organisation and I was struck by how numbers focused they were. The quote that we stated the chapter with (possibly from Einstein or Wilde) sprung to mind. On the one hand, one could set the participants up with a greater awareness of value, but it did make me wonder how ethical this might be if they went back to their organisation with confidence and articulation of a different position, only to be faced with the overwhelming odds of an ingrained culture. What I'm pointing at is that the process starts with that very early conversation that might unsettle both us and that individual, and which may well manifest itself in irritation, but one that we should take seriously.

What we are pointing to is a cultural unsettling that begins with us as OD practitioners, our clients and the participants. We list here a few quite reasonable questions and underlying anxieties:

- *Us as OD practitioners*: Why do some of us shy away from conversations about the impact our work has? What are the ways that we can describe and show impact that relates to the client's world? How can we tease out the underlying questions about impact and the assumptions that lie beneath them? And what impact will our understanding of impact have?
- *The client*: The client will have to have conversations with other people, perhaps her boss or the board. What will be the nature of these conversations? In particular, what counts for credible insights on which decisions can be made in that organisation? What actions might they take that will add value?
- *The participants*: In asking someone to give up their time to attend a workshop or a course, how can the scales be described that reasonably reflect the resource and time required in the present against the benefits, probably set into the future?

In other words, measuring impact is not just about numbers and previous success stories; it is more than that. It is about what we value and what those around us value and, in a circular way, is as much about OD as any of our other work.

Who's interested?

The question of who is interested in impact and at what point is important. It reflects the conversations that are being held in the organisation, in the context of everything else that is going on at the time and in relation to what counts as information. James reflects:

> A question I sometimes ask groups when I am talking about the impact of OD is who is interested in evaluating this impact at various stages of an OD project, from beginning to middle to end? Who actually cares about this? The answer I invariably get from OD people is something along the lines of: "At the beginning it is the CEO/HR Director and me. In the middle it is the people involved in the project and me. In the end, it is usually just me. Everyone else has either stopped caring or, more likely, has moved on, taken on another role, become preoccupied by another crisis or been sacked."

This view tends to be expressed in a rather pained or cynical tone. But seen as part of the wider pattern of conversations, concerns and muddle in organisations, it is perhaps to be expected.

This demonstrates one of the essential challenges we have in OD: we are measuring the ebbs, flows and the emergence of a living system of which we are part, rather than the outputs of a machine – even in the conversation with the client on issues of impact.

Comparing apples with pears

Gregory Bateson, who did much to shape systems theory and cybernetics in the twentieth century, provided the following insight:

> We have tried to build a bridge to the wrong half of the ancient dichotomy between form and substance. The conservative laws for energy and matter concern substance rather than form. But mental process, ideas, communication, organization, differentiation, pattern, and so on, are matters of form rather than substance.

> (Bateson, 1972, p.xxxii)

What Bateson is saying here, which we can apply to OD, is that we have a tendency to compare irreconcilable ideas; in other words, to compare apples with pears. Alongside the ideas themselves, the techniques to describe and measure them are similarly irreconcilable. And what is more, we seldom notice these fundamental category mistakes. The consequence is that we use the wrong techniques to measure the wrong phenomena and we ascribe the resultant insights to the wrong ways of knowing. Substance, in Bateson's terms, is just 'stuff', material things that we can handle, inspect and weigh. Form is about flows. These are inherently dynamic and thus change constantly. We need to be more precise and clear about which of these flows we are interested in, and how we relate to and use them.

Organisations seek profit, growth, new customers, markets, service delivery, quality, efficiency and so on. Many of these are tangible things that can be equated to the 'substance' world that Bateson is describing above: by 'tangible' we mean they can be measured. But from an OD point of view, let us consider the qualities that deliver these tangible things. These might be engagement, motivation, inspiration, emotional connection, dedication, caring or that ubiquitous yet monstrously ill-defined quality: leadership. So even behind the tangible we quickly find problems that defy neat description.

Heraclitus was getting at something similar when he said "one cannot step in the same river twice". The object of the river only exists to point to on a map or in the words we use. Its physical counterpart exists as water cuts its way down hillside, mountain and moor on its most efficient way to the sea. So we cannot experience this unique event of wading through this particular river other than once. The same is true in leadership development, for example. We talk about leaders, their development and the impact they have; but each leader is unique, as is the impact they have. We cannot say with any confidence that training X number of leaders according to Y learning objectives will not amount to Z impact. Returning to the river, our interaction between the object of the 'river' and its physical flowing counterpart needs to be treated with humility; they are not the same. By humility, we mean more than just caution between associating one with the other. We might ask ourselves, what are the contextual features by which we interpret and make judgement? What are the shortcuts we are making in these judgements and what other evidence should we look for? And what do these judgements and conversations say about us and the wider system of which we are part?

What we notice with our group of OD people, whose sponsors have moved on by the end of the project, is that they are simply noticing a likely flow that happens all the time in the dynamic, complex world of organisations. Bateson and his ilk are not saying, however, that measuring form is impossible. Instead, we might be going about it in an unhelpful way, such as by bringing in scientific assumptions of predictable cause and effect set against a backdrop where variables are known and static.

Perhaps we need a more helpful metaphor than the scientist in a white coat – how about a kaleidoscope? Each shard of coloured glass is some form of insight – a person's experience, some form of survey, a focus group or a reflexive conversation in the staff restaurant, how we come to understand the organisation, our own values and so on. But they are presented to us in our own kaleidoscope that we experience uniquely, where both the shards and the white space in between present us with an image in the movement. As we go about our work, the kaleidoscope twists, presenting us with new images and insights. These we discuss with others from which new insights emerge, as do themes that we can agree or disagree on. And from this we go on together, making decisions, taking actions and understanding our world differently. Seen in this way we still recognise measurement as being important, but we do so with humility, aware that the next conversation is a further step in that evaluation process.

This problem is not unique to OD. Indeed, the scientific world is equally riven with this confusion between form and substance, particularly when it comes to the world of living things. As Bateson said:

> In other words, logic and quantity turn out to be inappropriate devices
> for describing organisms and their interactions and internal
> organization.

> (Bateson, 1972, p.20)

The words we use to talk about the impact of OD and how we evaluate it can thus be problematic. Consider for example, the word 'benchmarking'. This is an engineering term and as such is entirely appropriate for the world of substance, but completely bogus in the world of form. How can you benchmark a river?

So we need to be careful and more confident to challenge the language of substance when it is applied to the world of OD. We need to shift the language towards things that flow but that can be described and tracked. We can, for example, consider flows in terms of difference and quality. These are two important measures that the OD practitioners can focus on. To quote Bateson's dictum: we are interested in the "difference that makes a difference".

To illustrate the evaluation of OD, James often shows this slide of his own street in London (see Figure 7.1).

Figure 7.1: James' street in London – the different facets of evaluation

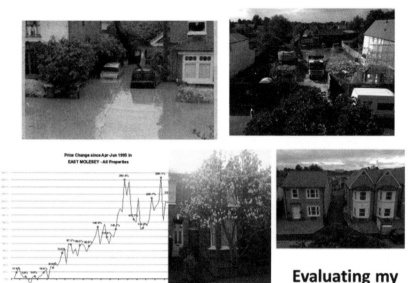

James reflects:

> This slide shows several photos of my road. The question I often ask is: what is the difference that makes a difference? Or to put it another way, what is the difference that matters?
>
> Is it:
>
> - The history of my street, which was flooded in 1968 (top left)
> - The quality of life when living opposite a building site (top right)
> - The architecture, when the building work has been completed (bottom right)
> - The house prices in my area (bottom left)
> - Preserving an ancient magnolia tree rather than chopping it down and turning it into a driveway, just so I can always park my car outside my house (middle bottom)?

The point here is not to judge which relationship matters but to *choose what has significant quality*. These qualities that matter to us can be consistently tracked. We can persistently pay attention to the difference that matters. So although we cannot stand in the same river twice, we can measure the quality of it from time to time. Knowing that this measurement will always be partial and subjective does not mean we shouldn't do it. They are just some of the coloured shards that make the picture.

The scientific to the emergent – some examples

In this section, we will explore two different perspectives of measuring impact. This first takes a scientific and positivist approach that explores the often unnoticed attraction to this way of analysis and its implications. We then move to a more emergent and relational example that takes a more hesitant view of measuring impact, but one that seeks to understand it in the wider organisational context.

Here Rob reflects on a recent workshop he attended:

> Recently, I was at a leadership forum with people from different sectors all interested in leadership evaluation, both from a practitioner and an academic perspective. In the morning, the second speaker gave an overview of his project. As a commissioner of a large number of leadership programmes he had developed a process of evaluation. This was in anticipation of the question: "what good are we doing?"
>
> What was created in considerable detail had the hallmark of a positivist mindset. I will now give an overview of the session. Note the delegates' response to this: they were enthusiastic about the process but didn't notice its implications, or even how it related to their own experience.
>
> The speaker took us through a number of sequential steps that were to be applied. These were to be clear as to what you want to achieve; what you are going to do (the intervention); what your 'theory of change' is; how you might measure impact; and finally, how you are to do the evaluation. In this case, the theory of change was the process by which leadership will occur and manifest itself.
>
> All of these steps would occur before the leadership development would start. Measures would be taken before, during and after. The assessment would be carried out on three levels: the organisation, the leader and the developer. Few programmes had actually been through this process; it was still early days. The process was deductive and involved applying the scientific paradigm mentioned earlier. In the room, there was much enthusiastic nodding and agreement that this was well designed and would add value. What was of value had to be pre-defined before the activity started. However, each person's leadership development within the cohort would be unique and take on its own emergent path shaped by the contexts experienced in relation to their values, abilities, drive and so forth.
>
> The story of the person sitting next to me made this clear. She had been a teacher and her boss had identified her as a person with the potential for being a secondary head teacher. A university course had been identified that was approved by the leadership body as fulfilling their defined leadership criteria. She described the leadership course as

enlightening, but it took her on a completely different path from that envisaged. She still works in education though. From a linear perspective, her head teacher or the evaluation team might describe this as a failure. From the perspective of wider education, it would be seen as a success: one of 'enabled serendipity'. The perspective or 'world view' is therefore important.

There are implications. Firstly, there was little awareness in the group of these contradictions, or of the opportunity and danger there was in being critically aware of one's 'world view'. In other words, how it shapes what we think is valuable. What was experienced was akin to a reflex action that is very common and fails to ask the question: if we look at the world this way, what are we not seeing? Secondly, there is little point in talking about the world as being dynamic, volatile, a system or using complexity ideas if we are drawn towards a linear means of describing it.

What can we make of this and what useful steps can we take? Within the field of OD, the question of the linkage between leadership development and organisational benefit has been the focus of much attention (Finney and Jefkins, 2009; Holbeche, 2012). In one paper on OD evaluation by the Roffey Park Institution, evaluation is defined broadly as "assessing the value, worth or merit of an intervention, programme or project" (Finney and Jefkins, 2009). Here, the authors make the point that practitioners tend to focus on both qualitative and quantitative factors (Finney and Jefkins, 2009; Francis et al., 2012) but this is understood in the rich context of the organisation and the actual project. The evaluation offers insight in terms of what is immediately 'seeable' – in other words, the woven fabric of the work done, the organisation, the people on the programme and the developers themselves. These scattered and occasionally irreconcilable insights are used in the service of the next move to be taken. Examples of this might include any adjustments to an OD programme, additional support and individual might need, how insights might come to affect a strategy being developed, and the commissioning of a new talent programme.

Rob reflects:

> A couple of years ago I was running a leadership programme for a healthcare organisation. Several dozen senior managers and consultant doctors went through an action-learning-based Post Graduate Certificate in Leadership and Management. The HR director, the CEO and others were interested in understanding its impact so they commissioned a management consultancy to carry out an evaluation. Following a number of interviews and analyses, the report came back giving examples of the programme's impact. There was also commentary that linked the impact of the individuals to the wider organisation, particularly with the leadership projects that they had

undertaken. The conversations I had with the HR director were interesting. She understood the context and the depth of the comments made by the interviewees (which were of course anonymous) in relation to what was going on in the organisation; what she was hearing in the voices of the interviewees was relatable to her experience.

This influenced other conversations with director colleagues and others, thus affecting further actions and understanding. Here the evaluation report was not *the* account of the programme, but one of a number of insights; some, like the report, were written artefacts whilst others took the form of conversations and the memories of those involved. It was a part of the temporal flow of sensemaking insight that they were part of, as opposed to a standalone snapshot. All of these added to the mix of how the organisation was run, an organisation that was seen as outstanding by the regulators. The story is more fully explored in a couple of papers I published with my colleagues (Warwick, McCray and Board, 2017; Warwick, McCray and Palmer, 2017).

These stories should not come as a surprise, but they are worth taking seriously. Returning to Finney and Jefkins (2009), one OD practitioner interviewed suggested the following rethink: "instead of using the words 'measurement' and 'evaluation', I prefer to use the word 'learning'" (Finney and Jefkins, 2009). This is telling and features in the literature more widely (Francis et al., 2012). This is seen in the context of wider organisational learning and impact, not only of those actively 'orchestrating' change processes but also those subject to the activities. It therefore stresses the emergent properties as people react, learn and go on as a socially heuristic process, as we saw in the second example. The issue of reflexivity is therefore critical – a process that was evident in the second example but absent in the first.

Whilst there is no linear cause and effect between leadership development and organisational outcome in a scientific sense, there are patterns of useful emergent insight. The weaving together of these fragments takes thought consideration as one senses what to do next in the rich context of the here and now – an ability that requires reflexivity, both individually within oneself and to engage in wider reflexive conversations with others.

Throwing ourselves into the mix: how we affect the picture

There is another complication, of course. This is because our relationship to these qualities and their differences won't remain the same when we take an interest in them. If we start to notice them, they make change *because* we notice them. The meaning and attention we give to things also changes them.

To illustrate this, we go back to OD's famous 'lightbulb moment' in Hawthorne, Illinois, in 1923. As Ben Goldacre, author of *Bad Science*, explains:

> I will give you the simplified 'myth' version of the findings, as a rare compromise between pedantry and simplicity. When the researchers increased light levels, they found that performance improved. But when they reduced the light levels, performance improved then, too. In fact, they found that no matter what they did, productivity increased anyway. This finding was very important: when you tell workers that they are part of a special study to see what might improve productivity and then you do something... they improve their productivity. This is a kind of placebo effect, because the placebo is not about the mechanics of a sugar pill, it is about the cultural meaning of an intervention, which includes, amongst other things, your expectations, and the expectations of the people tending to you and measuring you.
>
> (Goldacre, 2008, p.139)

This is now called the 'Hawthorne Effect' or the 'Observer Effect' and has important implications in OD. Even a passive act of watching comes to have an impact even in the most benign of conditions, as James explains.

> We have to be careful. I remember, one morning, as I toyed with some of the different ways we can 'cut the cake' of the world in front of us, I found myself in the restaurant of an hotel in Rugby, UK, watching the staff serving breakfast. I considered them, in their work, from the perspective of Frederick Winslow Tayor (1856–1925), one of the ancestors of OD. He dreamed of making organisational studies a true science of substances, to borrow Bateson's term. Putting on the spectacles of his scientific management worldview, I evaluated their work. I wondered, for example, on what basis the decision had been made (seemingly 'right' in my view) to have four of them on duty. It seemed about enough; they could all be attentive enough, without over-staffing. I took a mechanical view of their work, as a process to be engineered.
>
> I then considered the scene from a motivational perspective, wondering about the 'hygiene factors', the baseline requirements needed to get effort out of them, such as pay and reward (Herzberg, 1968). Then I thought about the 'motivational factors' that might be needed to eke out that crucial, extra bit of discretionary effort. What data would I collect about this?
>
> Next I considered them from the perspective of Barry Oshry's *Seeing Systems* (Oshry, 1995) and I wondered how they might configure themselves as 'Tops', 'Middles', 'Bottoms' and 'Customers'. I also wondered, borrowing from the perspective James C. Scott, what data I could dig out, if I really looked for it, that might demonstrate their 'hidden transcripts' of rebellion (Scott, 1990). For example, what graffiti

might I find on the staff toilet walls? I wondered about the quality of their smile and how genuine it was, considering the perspective of Arlie Russell Hochschild, and how she critiqued the way in which corporations tried to colonise the emotions of their workers (Hochschild, 2003).

So I considered several different ways of capturing the qualities that might matter to me. Indeed, if we imagine the scene in front of me as some kind of flow, then we move away from considering 'data' (which suggests qualities of fixed inert substances that can be measured) towards a new term, 'capta', which suggests that we in fact tend to draw a circle around the particular parts of the dynamic world we are choosing to focus on. 'Data' comes from the Latin root 'dare' meaning 'to give', whereas 'capta' comes from 'capere' meaning 'to take'. It therefore recognises that the distinctions we make in (or take from) the world do actually matter.

Indeed, even mainstream scientific researchers are more frequently using it as a term. For example, the archaeologist, Christopher Chippindale, writes:

Is the customary word 'data' a good name for archaeological records and facts? 'Data' means the things that are 'given', but archaeological observations and facts are never given at all. Rather, they are captured by the researcher, who seeks to grasp from the material record the essentials of some complex and little-known phenomenon, often remote in time and usually ambiguous in material expression. We should prefer to use the better word 'capta', the things that have been captured, and to realise that this word captures the essence of what we do.

(Chippindale, 2000, p.605)

But as we return to James, events now starting to involve him in unexpected ways.

But as I mused on all of this, what happened next in that breakfast scene was chastening. These waitresses (and they were all women) had noticed me noticing them. This seemed to have an impact on them, making them (understandably) self-conscious and even slightly embarrassed. Before I knew it, I had (thoughtlessly) made an impact, even a dent, in their world, by turning them into a kind of object in mine. This taught me about impact most profoundly.

In summary, we are part of the evaluation and come to affect what is 'real' for all of us. This can be useful but it is not without its political effect, which we will now explore.

Value, evaluation and recognising the positives of what we do

In the poem 'Our Greatest Fear', Marianne Williamson (b.1951) begins "It is our light, not our darkness that most frightens us". The point she is making is that we have impact, and sometimes we are uncomfortable in recognising this and demonstrating it to others. We should recognise and celebrate that we can and often do bring about positive change.

The word 'evaluation' has the same root as 'value'; but whilst the latter implies something that is precious and sought after, the former is more sinister, something to be cautious of, to keep at a distance from. What if we were to see 'evaluation' in a more positive light? Perhaps that might make us bolder and prouder of our work. And even more imaginative and free thinking about how we might go about evaluation, including bringing in the voices of the different people we work with, as well as our own. An important first step is finding out what different people mean by the word 'value' before jumping to 'evaluation'. In short, it is the opportunity we have to bring the two words 'evaluation' and 'value' together and, in so doing, to recognise our own role more positively.

Here is an example from James:

> My favourite tale of evaluation comes from when I worked on a customer service programme for a council, with dinner ladies (as they called themselves), people who prepared and served lunches to school children. Management had all sorts of clever ways of measuring customer satisfaction. Graphs and tables were prepared, yet these women seemed unmoved. So I asked them how they knew if they had delivered a quality service. They replied: "That's easy! It's how full the bin is at the end of lunch."

> Sometimes I think we believe that evaluation needs to look 'science-y', rather than human-scale. The point is that evaluation should involve both. To the managers, the graphs and bar charts had meaning. That's how evaluation needed to be packaged for them, in their language. But to the dinner ladies, quality looked like an empty bin. Our role is to make the connections between what different constituencies or tribes value (and hospitals are full of tribes) and how they speak about it.

So the steps in understanding what is of value are important and need careful consideration before we jump to the empty bin or the neat graph. And in this case, this will include the views of the school children.

So if measuring isn't hard, why do we find it difficult? Perhaps we don't think we're being 'science-y' enough? Or is it because if we evaluated what we did, we would reveal some uncomfortable truths about the organisation? Or because, deep down, we might be scared that we really do make a difference, as Williamson says.

It is revealing that OD is sometimes caricatured as being about the 'pink and fluffy' stuff. Is this a defence against what we might be giving voice to? The hard stuff that matters is: what are we doing, why are we doing it and what are the implications?

Here is an example of what happens when the question of what is of value becomes distant from those affected, which in turn drives the process of evaluation. Although we venture from the traditional mainstay of OD, pay attention to how decisions were taken, who was involved, who was excluded and the long-term implications. The case is taken from James C. Scott's book *Seeing Like a State* (Scott, 1998).

The nineteenth century saw a revolution in German forestry. Up until that point, the local government was content to levy taxes on the landowners and allow them to manage as they pleased. The forests had remained largely the same year on year, coping with natural disasters, fire, drought, flood, pests and everything else that nature and man had in mind. For the people, the forest wasn't just a source of timber, it was a mainstay of the economy.

Foliage was used as fodder, thatch and fruits were a source of food for animals and humans, twigs and branches were used as bedding and fencing, bark and roots was used for tanning – and the list goes on. Then the state took a more active interest in how forests were to be managed. Understandably, as people remote from the culture and the goings-on of the forest, they were only interested in lumber and this became *the* measure of success. Very quickly, impressive strides were made in identifying the 'right crop' (in this case Norwegian Spruce) and how this should be planted. The forests were cleared of undergrowth and line upon line of trees was planted. This became the visible sign of a well-managed forest and had an important symbolic meaning that struck a chord with industrialisation of the time. Yields of lumber increased dramatically and the method took off across the world.

Yields of timber in second- and third-generation forests dwindled, however. Second-generation production was 20–30% less than the first and a new word entered the vocabulary: *Waldsterben* (forest death). The soil became barren, without vital micro-nutrients and wildlife. The local economy suffered from the loss of sundry materials for livestock and inhabitants. The monoculture (in the sense both of species *and* of trees the same age) made them vulnerable to disease, storm and fire. It became a disaster, but one driven by 'sensible intent'.

The people in the central state lost sight of the richer picture of what was of value; they only saw this in their terms of measureable yield. The affected communities were not heard or understood, nor was local knowledge of the delicate and interconnected ecosystem.

The point we have been keen to explore in this section is the importance of the interconnection between value and evaluation and our role in shaping this connection in the conversations we can have with the different constituencies that we work with. As part of this, we should be proud of our work and contribution; only by doing this will others share their stories and explain what is of value to them. And in so doing, we can develop Lewin's legacy.

The questions this chapter invites

- Why are we interested in 'evidence' of impact? Who is interested and what are the underlying reasons for this interest? What are the underlying questions of 'impact' that we are missing?
- In a world of 'big data' that is increasingly interconnected with the many aspects of our lives, how will we give voice to the hesitant, imaginative and creative ways that we sense and interpret the world with other people?

A world of increasingly sophisticated machine learning brings into sharp focus the fundamental questions that are hard to understand; in summary, why are we doing what we are doing? It is thus not the answer that becomes important, it is the question. These are deeper and more philosophical issues that we must ponder before we consider 'impact'. These are political and contested tasks that require reflexive, listening and communicative abilities. Impact and evaluation will be increasingly relevant but only when considered alongside deeper contextual knowledge of the situation and people.

Photo: © Steve Marshall, www.drstevemarshall.com, @drstevemarshall

Reflexive practice and social ripples

Introduction

B EING REFLEXIVE IS A deep form of reflection on our actions and thoughts as part of a process of continual learning. Discussions on reflexivity have usually focused on the individual, but what if we were to think in more social terms? For example, we respond to gestures from others (conversations, emails, body language, the situation where these occur and so on) as others respond to ours, and in these interactions we craft realities from which we further build. Thought of in this way, we and others create and are affected by ripples within an organisation. Being reflexive enables us to notice, change course, ask fundamental questions – to get out of the rut. This is a deep form of organisational change. It affects us as OD practitioners, those that we work with in our practice and others who we may never meet but are affected by what we do. Our lives are not just about work: we have families and we are part of a community, all of whom come to affect who we are and what we bring to our work.

What we mean by reflexivity

Influenced by the work of the pragmatist philosopher George Herbert Mead, Frederick Steier explained that reflexivity can be thought of as 'bending back on itself' (Steier, 1991). There is an important real-time dynamic of thought, action and consequence. This melds with the social interaction one is part of and is influenced by intuition, tacit knowledge of the past and how one imagines a future. This can have both positive or negative consequences, as it addresses beliefs, ways of being and taken-for-granted assumptions (Cunliffe, 2009) and thus frequently unsettles. Indeed, sociologist Melvin Pollner describes reflexivity as "an 'unsettling', i.e. an insecurity regarding the basic assumptions, discourse and practices in describing reality" (Pollner, 1991). Although it is a feature of being a person, as we look around us, we know that some people are more attuned and able than others. That is not to say that the die is cast; it is an ability that can be further developed.

In this chapter, we explore reflexivity in three ways. Firstly, individually considering what it means for our thought and practice and how this comes to further affect what we do. Secondly, as we become interwoven within the fabric of others – for example, our clients and the teams we work with. And finally, at a meta-level, holistically as these meld together in the groups and communities of which we are part. But of course, all three are part of the whole.

There are choices as to what we pay attention to, both for ourselves and more loosely for others in the conversations that we initiate. But this comes with risk. Being reflexive can be transformative and has implications for others: what if this change takes us somewhere we did not want to travel? Suppose we were happier doing the same job day in, day out. As Morpheus explains to Neo in *The Matrix*, there are irreversible choices when it comes to our reality (Wachowski and Wachowski, 1999):

> You take the blue pill, the story ends. You wake up in your bed and believe whatever you want to believe. You take the red pill, you stay in Wonderland, and I show you how deep the rabbit hole goes.

These are serious, ethical considerations and ones that we can only sense and explore in the conversations we have, but for which we have no definitive answers.

The holistic nature of being reflexive

Reflexivity is not simply an intellectual pursuit, it relates to the entirety of who we are. To explore this we introduce the work of the French philosopher Michel Serres and others. We are interested in journeys, those that we have in learning and of interacting with others. Learning that changes us feels uncomfortable; it feels edgy and takes us to new places from which we cannot return. This hits us logically: we can form a rational case as to what happened, why and its future implications. However, there are emotional implications too for how we as well as others see ourselves in this movement. Serres takes a refreshing view with implications for reflexivity, our practice as OD practitioners and those we interact with.

Rarely when people refer to reflexivity do they consider the nature of the entire self as a physical, corporal, thinking and feeling being. These 'factors' are who we are and it would be wrong to ignore them: they affect our beliefs, and in turn our beliefs affect our decisions and our decisions affect those around us, just as other people's decisions affect us.

This is hard work. There is an irony that one of the most-cited books on reflexivity in research, *Reflexive Methodology – New Vistas for Qualitative Research* (Alvesson & Skoldberg, 2009), does not address the authors' own development; instead, the subject is addressed solely as an intellectual exercise at arm's length. This is not at all unusual.

We turn to Michel Serres, a French historian, mathematician, philosopher and traveller. His approach does not rely on sequential argument, carefully building one intellectual block on another; instead, it is synthetic and comparative, encouraging us to have a more embodied relationship with our world. It is a way of understanding what is aligned with reflexive engagement of how we come to make sense of experience. He is interested in the interactions between different ways of knowing, how these rub along and create new knowledge. He is sceptical that language and logical argument are capable of explanation alone; he draws on poetry, story and music. Here he explains in his typically poetic language how clever people get straight to the intellectual point but miss the bigger picture:

> I recall hearing philosophers in dialogue, screeching and quarrelling at the foot of beautiful mountains, on ocean beaches, in front Niagara Falls, they had the fixed gaze of those with something to say... they saw neither the snow of the glacier, nor the sea, they heard nothing of the crashing water, they were arguing... Dangerous people...

> (Steyaert, 2014, p.599)

For Serres, all five senses are important, not just those that we jump to without thought. And in this respect, our cleverness can outsmart us, can draw us down a narrow path where we feel most comfortable and expert. There are two interconnected questions: what is it we can do to develop a greater appreciation of what surrounds us? And how do we find a way to describe our learning that pays attention to this? In considering the first question, what might be the role of art, music and even poetry? In previous chapters we have discussed OD in terms of art and craft, so we explore this in relation to being reflexive. Music has a way of connecting us in multiple emotional ways as a means of amplifying and expanding our understanding rather than focusing and reducing, as is the case is a clever argument. For example, take Sergei Prokofiev's 1936 work for children, *Peter and the Wolf*. Early on, the narrator explains that Peter opens the gate and goes into the meadow. But it is only in the music that we connect with Peter's experience: a warm summer's day, running over tall dry unmown grass with its characteristic smell, being happy. In the chapter 'Knowledge, knowing and learning', we discussed Robert Grave's poem 'In Broken Images'. When describing action learning, it is difficult to put into words what holistic sense of experience a person should make themselves available to; but a poem seems able to do this.

In looking at the second question of how we describe our learning, Serres draws on the metaphor of swimming across a river. As we plunge into the river we hold onto the nearest bank. We experience the cold and gasp for breath, our peripheral circulation contracts and blood is directed to our inner core. As we start swimming we leave the safely of the shore behind and we are at risk of drowning and of succumbing to the cold, but we trust our body to do what it should: to survive. We feel the water around our body and we listen to our splashing, we notice as we put one arm in front of another and move our feet to reach the other bank. Once there, we seek the gravel under our feet and we climb out. But in so doing, we are changed, there is no going back to the person we were. The tutor can only take the person to the water's edge and offer encouragement, but it is in the disorientation of the in-between, of being in the middle of the river, that we learn, as Serres explains:

> In crossing the river, in delivering itself completely naked to belonging to the opposite shore, it has learned a third thing. The other side, new customs, a new language, certainty. But above all, it has just discovered learning in this blank middle that has no direction from which to find all directions. ... a place /milieu where all directions come together.

(Serres, 1991, p.7)

Rob gives an example of an experience, of a type which plays out every day. On the one hand, dealing with difficult situations and power can be role-played and written about. However, it is only in lived experience that its entirety can be felt with its fear, rapid sensemaking and judgement.

> Although this occurred many years ago, it is a situation that still makes me anxious when I recount it. I worked for an NHS organisation on a project in collaboration with a prestigious UK university. I was new to the role and was advising on the management of a laboratory that handled dangerous viruses, with frequent deliveries of new samples from Africa. I was due to meet the Principle Investigator, a Chinese American woman married to a French man. I say this because of the important cultural cues that were present, but that I missed. We got onto the issue of who was responsible for what and an argument started. The person stood up and approached where I was sitting, with a raised voice, speaking faster and faster, her body language getting more aggressive.
>
> This shocked me. The stakes increased when she picked up the phone explaining that she was calling the CEO I worked for, a person who was

South American, quite volatile, and someone I was wary of. Outwardly, I probably seemed quite calm – I'm like that – but inside I was panicking, I felt my face getting red. The room and my interaction with the person were hyperreal – noise, colours and smell were vivid. Although I felt immersed in the situation, I managed to detach myself, too. And in this I found my voice and was able to put my case with a clarity that surprised me as I was listening to myself saying those words. The incident was over in thirty minutes and we came to an agreement some time later on the way forward.

Here Rob was plunged in the water that Serres poetically describes, quickly having to catch his breath and find his way across to the other side. Rob explains the impact of this:

I became intrigued by power and the emotion of power that I had been subject to; and also, by the international culture that I saw at play. I started having conversations with people affected by this and new and fascinating stories emerged that would not be out of place in a political thriller (in fact, some of the people did serve time in prison). I became fascinated by the stories of how these relationships developed over the decades. In the course of my job, I got to know some of the people involved well and came to like many (but not all) of them. Outwardly confident and intelligent people gradually talked about tentative and less-secure parts of who they were and how past and present relationships were playing on their minds. My faith in rationality had been tested, but other ways of understanding were emerging for me. And as I became more confident and understanding of power and relationships, I became able to anticipate difficult situations, and to prepare myself and those around me. I was developing an intuition that I'm still drawing on. It is an intuition that I now hardly notice in practice, but as I think of that incident I am back there in a flash along with my raised heart rate.

We hear of the long-term implications of reflexive learning and how this rippled out and affected others. The pattern of conversations and how people related to each other had changed. In an imaginary conversation explaining that knowledge, akin to a harlequin's coat, occurs at the interface between the fragments, Serres states:

Just as the body... assimilates and retains various differences experienced during travel and returns home a half-breed of new gestures and other customs, dissolved in the body's attitudes and functions, to the point that it believes... nothing has changed, so the secular miracle of tolerance, of benevolent neutrality welcomes, in peace just as many apprenticeships in order to make the liberty of invention, thus of thought, spring forth from them.

(Serres, 1991, p.xvii)

Here we see that knowledge does not form from discreet blocks, but occurs in unsettling interactions that become unnoticed as they become a part of us. And from this we are changed as we interact with others.

We have sought in this section to lay the ground for considering reflexivity in a holistic sense that pays attention to us as a full person, one enmeshed in the lives of others. In this way of talking about reflexivity, words are not enough – but they are all we have here.

Practical steps

In the following sections, we address the question: what can we practically do to affect reflexivity? There are two interlinking hopes: firstly, that reflexivity will increase; and secondly, that there will be positive personal and organisational impact. But these cannot be guaranteed.

Being reflexive

A first step in being reflexive is to be open to taking one's experience seriously. What are the hidden assumptions and ways of doing things that we take for granted and give little thought to? The French sociologist and anthropologist Pierre Bourdieu provided the following example to illustrate this:

> When you read, in Saint-Simon, about the quarrel of hats (who should bow first), if you were not born in a court society, if you do not possess the habitus of a person of the court, if the structures of the game are not also in your mind, the quarrel will seem futile and ridiculous to you. If, on the other hand, your mind is structured according to the structures of the world in which you play, everything will seem obvious and the question of knowing if the game 'is worth the candle' will not even be asked.

> (Bourdieu, 1998, p.77)

Imagine yourself as a member of a royal court: the issues of respect, power and ritual are vital in how people relate to each other and how things get done. The doffing of a hat in the wrong order or with too little or too much flourish matters; it could lead to exclusion or erosion of influence. To the courtiers, such rituals will go unnoticed and as such are undiscussable. The question is: what are the rituals we follow today and what is their importance in helping us to achieve our goals? We therefore have a double reflexive bind: on the one hand, we might accept that we need to explore our experience seriously; but on the other, this is hard to do given how we are so enmeshed in our situation. In short, how does a fish become aware of the water in which it is swimming?

One way to extricate ourselves from this bind is to enlist the support of others who are not part of those relations and do not have a stake in the outcome. We need someone who can ask the challenging and naïve question.

Of course, we are not only talking about obscure historical forms of French society; this is universal. The ethnographer Karen Ho provides a vivid account of this in her book *Liquidated – An Ethnography of Wall Street* (Ho, 2009). Here she describes the dysfunctional systemic dynamic between elite universities in the US and Wall Street banks and how their actions come to affect society as a whole, particularly how this has impacted job security. In a short narrative, at a micro-scale one male banker reflected on coming to work as a junior analyst wearing braces. He had crossed an unwritten line by suggesting to colleagues he spent too much time in the morning getting dressed: "You are supposed to look good but not overly so" (Ho, 2009, p.73). This was something for Vice Presidents and above. Later, a female banker reflected on what she wore, particularly her shoes, and how this came to affect how her mainly male colleagues perceived her. This was important as she felt it would come to influence her appointment on future prestigious projects (Ho, 2009, p.118). These small details matter and provide a fascinating window into an organisation's culture if only we notice them – a difficult task for the internal change consultant.

To start the process, we might ask what stories are we telling ourselves and others, and what are the short cuts that we make? Often, it is in the short cuts that our assumptions can be found. And from our assumptions there is a way into being more reflexive. We are not talking of the heroic or extraordinary, quite the reverse: we are interested in the mundane. Examples might include:

- *Decision making*. Who is involved in making a decision and who is excluded? What of race and gender? What type of evidence is seen as holding more sway – do people look for tables, graphs and numbers or do people like a crafted argument from a senior person? Are they made quickly or subject to lengthy deliberation? Also, where are decisions made – in formal settings, with minute takers and terms of reference, or are they made on the hoof?
- *A report*. Linked to the above, in preparing a paper for a board meeting, say, what are the conventions about its style, length and approval? Again, do people look for graphs and figures?
- *Gossip (or what some call 'water-cooler moments')*. How does informal information flow around the organisation and what are the gatherings where this occurs? What does this say to you about centres of power – might this be centralised at the top or more distributed? What do people talk about and what metaphors might they use to describe their experience? Do people talk of being frightened, of being proud or of having love for their work?

- *The political.* When you need to get something done, who do you lobby and talk to? What preparation do you do and how do you approach them – and do you make it seem accidental, a chance brush past in a corridor? How do others approach you? Do you anticipate your boss's next question and move and seek to resolve it?
- *Speaking to other people.* Even the routines of the travel to and from work, having lunch, or how we move around the workplace offer reflexive possibilities by leading to encounters with different people and having different conversations. Even the process of seeing, hearing and feeling differently enables us to experience the word afresh.
- *What you wear.* What choices do you make about your personal appearance? What do you wear and why? What messages are you conveying with this?

These are just some broad examples from which the question 'why?' can be asked. There will be others. But this is something you cannot fully do yourself. As with the court of Saint-Simon, it takes others who can work with your experience afresh. And to explore we need stories, either in our minds or written down, for example as a narrative. A narrative written down close to the point of the events occurring will not fade as our memory does. At that particular point, when we are facing a difficult situation when a decision is needed, multiple possibilities are present (Warwick and Board, 2013). Once that decision has been taken and time has passed, we see our situation through the lens of the certainty, in other words, of post-hoc rationalisation.

In exploring our experience, what might we pay attention to? The logic of how we go about our work is important and includes how we trace the steps we have taken in our mind and our response to others. However, we are more than intellectual rational beings. We also need to consider our emotional and physi-ological response too: for example, our anxiety, doubt and even love. Or in recalling a painful situation where we lost face, the quickening of our heart and reddening of our face, for example. Consider too instinct and hunches as we swiftly move from one topic to focus in on another; why is this so and what are we not paying attention to? What are the short cuts we make so as to make our working life achievable and efficient? How are these shortcuts helping us and what are they blinding us to? All of these factors are parts of our reflexive mix.

Encouraging reflexivity: encouraging others

In the above section we discussed the nature of reflexivity and the prompts and questions we can ask ourselves to enhance our own reflexive abilities. We can use this understanding with others as well, for example, in coaching or in action learning. It is not our intention to discuss these here in any depth, but in taking the example of action learning we will highlight how the principles and practices enhance reflexivity.

Action learning is the development of the individual by working on problems that matter to them. Reg Revans, who is often described as the father of action learning, stated that there can be no learning without action and no action without learning (Revans, 1998). Action learning is a process that provides a grounded context from which the participant can learn whilst doing. It comprises several learners with an experienced facilitator (Pedler, 2011). Here the participants are supported to provide both challenge and support to each other to enable each to see their problem from a different perspective. With this new insight they then agree some form of action, the results of which will be discussed at the next meeting. Action learning impacts on the wider organisation as actions and conversations inspired by the learning set come to ripple out beyond the set itself (Warwick, McCray and Palmer, 2017). We now address some of the principles of action learning that are also more widely applicable to reflexivity in general.

A learning must feel safe. Ground rules are established by the participants, the most important of which is often confidentiality. People need to be able to speak as freely as they feel to be possible to address their problem (although this can never be absolute). Speaking freely is a precondition enabling the process mutual noticing and engagement in each other's experience. This does not materialise on day one and is something that the facilitator will draw attention to.

Creating the safe conditions provides the enabling context for supportive and challenging conversations. These are conversations based on open questions rather than offering solutions. A well-chosen question has the ability to stick with the individual long after the conversation has finished. It prompts the deeper question 'why?' and hence the noticing and making available for discussion of assumptions and unnoticed routines and practices.

It is from these conversations that action can be agreed, the impact of which can be discussed at the next meeting. Not everything goes well, of course: reactions can be negative as well as positive as the ripples come to have impact. This is not to say that this is necessarily bad: negative reactions can often lead to acute moments of learning.

The temporal nature of process is therefore important. This allows the participant to notice the changes in the development of their thought and practice. Not only this, but it also enables them to reflect on how these changes have been reacted to socially, amongst their teams, boss, clients, family and friends, and so on.

You, we, I: together forming and being formed

Drawing on the above, in this section we direct attention to the social nature of reflexivity and how our actions and thoughts come to affect others, as indeed others come to affect us. Here we show the wider impacts that reflexivity can have. We start with an example from James. Here we notice the reflexive realisation a leader has for their own abilities and weaknesses in a changing situation and how the actions of this person come to affect others.

> The R&D department of a bioengineering company was headed up by a woman who had been at the company a long time. She has many good relationships across the business and this was reflected in her reputation. A number of interesting new potential projects were being developed in the department, some of which were potentially exciting. But as she knew, it was early days and she had to keep things going – or in her words "keep the roof up" – so that the researchers could continue to play in the space she had been instrumental in creating. She knew full well how she was regarded by her boss and the rest of the executive team. She was willing to be patronised by him and his colleagues if that's what it took. The way they talked down to her pushed her buttons, but she was able to contain her exasperation because she knew that getting hot under the collar was in fact just the excuse that one or two of the more sceptical executive directors needed to create waves and shut her down. Every time it looked like a reckoning would be coming and her budget cut, or things would be reorganised to the detriment of the department, she was prepared to fight her corner and lobby with just the right people so that she could out manoeuvre any threat. Meanwhile, she was also nurturing a deputy who, she hoped, could take over when she would retire, a prospect she longed for. But she wasn't prepared to go until she knew that the department's future was secure.
>
> Her deputy was quite a different type of person. He was a tall man, in contrast to her petite frame. He was ex-military and was very aware that this meant people treated him quite differently. They expected him, in his own words, to "have it together much more than I do"!
>
> Meanwhile, the scene was changing. An economic downturn meant that the company needed an injection of capital to stay afloat. A buyer from overseas approached the board. One of the reasons they looked with interest at the company was because of the reputation of the R&D department. The department head, however, realised that this new company had an ethos that she wouldn't fit into. A great people person, highly astute and intuitive, she wasn't a great organiser or systems manager. She relied on people, as she put it, "to sort out the spreadsheets, whilst I do the talking". She knew that the buyer would want her to make sense of the systems in a way which was beyond her capability or interest. She saw her moment to leave and she took it.

"It's your time", she said to her deputy, as they stood sharing a quiet moment over a glass of wine at her leaving party.

The deputy understood how he was seen by the new regime. In his view, they were disproportionately impressed by his military background. But he was prepared to use this image to the benefit of the department. He was a good organiser and someone who knew his way around a spreadsheet. He was good at presenting information in a way he knew the new senior team would appreciate. It was also good timing because the products that the department had been working on were starting to become commercially viable. He was able to manage the transition to viable production, and convince the senior team that the investment would yield returns, even though he couldn't be sure that they would. He spoke their language.

After a year, the former manager and deputy met for a dinner to catch up and discuss how life had turned out. They reflected on how they had, mostly with great serendipity, been the right leaders for the department at the right times.

"I would never have been able to nurture its small beginnings like you did," he said.

"And I would never have been able to take it to the next stage like you," she responded. "It's as if the department knew the type of leadership it needed. All we had to do was realise what our own strengths and weaknesses were, and how they fitted, or not, with the changing status quo."

This is a story of organisational change and how a leader, once capable and understanding of her former domain, comes to realise that she does not have the personal attributes for the future of the organisation. In doing so, she has reached out and had conversations with those that might be better placed, despite their own reservations. Kenneth Tucker, in his book on the work of the sociologist Anthony Giddens, makes the following point on the relationship between the erosion of tradition and how we reflexively respond to this:

In the late modern context, traditions lose their taken-for-granted status. That they must be rationally defended furthers the crisis of industrial society, which extends to its very basis of legitimacy. Social reflexivity expands, creating a gulf between knowledge and social control. This situation leads to a greater sense of social and personal risk and to more emphasis on bottom-up decision-making and flexible production.

(Tucker, 1998, p.147)

In this example and Tucker's reflection on Giddens, we can appreciate now more than ever the changing nature of our organisational lives. Added to this, the certainties that we once took for granted are quickly becoming eroded. As we saw in the example, how we reflexively understand ourselves and others becomes increasingly important. But this came with risk for both individuals in the story: would they succeed in their new roles? How did others relate to them? How do they now see their own identity? How prepared are they for their next roles? What sense do they now make of the future? And so on. There is no risk-free option.

In the previous section, we explored some characteristics of action learning in relation to reflexivity. Here we develop this with an example that affected the individual with implications that rippled through the organisation. We see the development of an individual's reflexive abilities in relation to their impact on the organisation; a growing confidence and ability; and how they too are impacted by organisational dynamics.

Rob explains:

> A couple of years ago I was facilitating a learning set of senior NHS managers and consultant doctors. One individual had expertise in a particular surgical technique. Although it had yet to be implemented in the hospital, elsewhere it had been shown to lead to better clinical outcomes and cost. Her previous attempts at implementing the procedure had led to resistance and objections from different clinical disciplines and the operations side of the hospital. They cited different and frequently changing objections to her idea, which was leading to frustration. Early in the learning set, she would talk about this with an exclamation of: "why don't they understand... ?" In the ten sessions that we were together, the nature of the conversation changed. The people in her learning set posed questions that made her see the situation differently and from the perspective of others. And in doing this she came to understand her own perspective and assumptions in greater depth. She was developing an understanding of the power dynamics and politics of the hospital beyond her own department. In her department she had direct control over events, but over the wider hospital she could only have influence. The actions that she agreed to take in the learning set were reported at subsequent meetings. It was clear that these conversations and actions were impacting others and enabling them to see their world differently, too. The questioning she was subject to in the learning set was used by her to understand the objections and problems of other people. These objections were understood and steps to build confidence and agreement were determined. As we came to the end of our time together, the surgical operation in question was starting to become routine. The patterns of how people related and understood each other had changed – and she had been promoted.

> (Warwick, McCray and Palmer, 2017)

What is interesting in this story is its subject's confidence. She started off being very confident and assured about her own position, but confused as to why others didn't see its value. This soon shifted and she became less sure of her position. But she was also curious and could see, with the questioning of those around her, how she might make useful next steps. And as she acted, others responded to this in ways that enabled further change to happen. Her ability to notice organisational politics had developed as had her understanding of her own position within the figuration of power relationships. Although this unsettled her, she was more able to see, negotiate and move through the objections and resistance that caused her frustration. Here we can use the analogy of the glass wall. By being unreflexive, individuals repeatedly hit their head on the unseen and unnoticed. Greater reflexivity cannot eliminate this but at least it prepares people to move and to work out where the gaps and doors are.

Siren calls of un-reflexive reflexivity

It is important not to unreflexively fall into the trap that reflexivity is a solution for all people and problems. Is the call to be more reflexive right for everyone and every role? Let's consider an extreme personal example. Rob reflects:

> Shortly after leaving university I had a temporary job in a banana ripening factory where boxes of bananas were unloaded and stacked in large ventilation rooms to ripen the fruit. Each day the work was to load and unload shipping containers full of bananas. It was hard physical work. However, people there seemed very happy with good camaraderie. Several of them had been there for over twenty years. I was amazed, thinking "How could anyone stand this?" After a few days they offered me a full-time job – perhaps they could see potential!

In encouraging greater reflexivity, perhaps with the agenda 'there is more to life than…', how might the conversations flowed? What might be said and how might this be responded to? It would probably be seen as patronising, viewed with bemusement and ridicule. One or two might be interested and be prompted to explore new avenues and have different conversations. Either way, there was a risk of naively blundering in and causing hurt. Although this case might be unusual for an OD practitioner, it does shine a light on the importance of relationships between the group and the inquisitive newcomer.

The counter point is increasingly true: a number of professions, such as nursing and medicine, require people to be reflective (Schön, 1991), to write journals and think carefully about their practice. Here the agenda is to improve practice, learning from both mistakes and what went well.

In these two cases, there are a number of issues to consider: whose voice is given primacy? Who is being marginalised and who is this benefiting? As with any intervention, it cannot be assumed that asking these questions is necessarily good and will lead to positive results. From an organisation's perspective, what might the practical consequences be if staff frequently challenged taken-for-granted norms? For many organisations this would be vital, but not for all. Alvesson and Spicer address this question in their frequently cited paper on functional stupidity (Alvesson and Spicer, 2012). Here they explore an important tension. On the one hand, the efficiency of groups un-reflectively working in the same pattern of relationships and not challenging each other; and on the other, the potential in new ways of working and the impact on innovation that comes with reflexive thought and mutual challenge. They do not offer any solution other than a meta-reflexivity of those that can affect those relationships.

For individuals, reflexive questions might be unsettling and challenging to self and identity. In a change of thought and practice, the individual may also come to be seen differently by colleagues. Sometimes this will be a change for the good, but this cannot be guaranteed.

The question that needs to be addressed is this: who is the beneficiary and who might be marginalised and negatively affected? This forms a part of our own reflexive craft, with similar questions asked of ourselves.

The questions this chapter invites

- What are our organisational practices that we take for granted?
- What questions might we ask to encourage social noticing of our thought and practice?
- What are the risks to others and ourselves in doing this?

We can distinguish reflexivity from reflection: sometimes with the latter there isn't any learning or change. In fact, sometimes we reflect in order to reinforce our prejudices rather than look for the mote in our own eye. As we will see in the next chapter, Jas Porter had to face the gap between his stated values and his prejudices. For him, these only emerged in the everyday practice of change in support of diversity – not on the conference platform but in a walk around a lake. We can't legislate for our lack of insight, but we can recognise ourselves in the midst of it and respond to that insight. We will have to develop greater resilience and trust in order to cope collectively. Otherwise, the likely dislocation and fragmentation may lead to unhelpful or even ugly patterns of behaviour. OD folk will lead the vanguard of resilience if we continue to engender reflexivity in others; but first and foremost, we must demonstrate it in and of ourselves.

Photo: © Steve Marshall, www.drstevemarshall.com, @drstevemarshall

9

How the 2048 world of Jas Porter and Imogen Sharp helps us think about OD today

We don't see the world as it is, but as we are.

The Talmud

A S WE DEVELOPED THIS book together, we also went on a parallel, imaginal journey. We hypothesised that we needed a creative device to stimulate our thinking, as well as make the book less dry. Our lives, like most, are lived in a habitual workaday rhythm, filled with mundane details. If the process of OD and change needs to artful, as we have argued, then how to break out of this sleepwalk of the everyday? Perhaps waking up from the dream is about creating new ones? In life and in OD, imagination might be what saves us.

Using our imagination to break out of the mundane isn't a new idea in the organisational context:

> In the late 1970s Sperry Univac, a large IT company, sponsored a series
> of seminars exploring the potential social consequences of
> contemporary science fiction with a view to enhancing their product
> development...

(Smith et al., 2001)

So for you the reader and for us the authors, the imaginative devices we use are intended as a playground for our thoughts. This resonates with the idea of OD practitioners as workplace story tellers, 'Mercurians' as Slezkine might put it (see Chapter 4). Isn't our work always about helping people find meaning together? That's what stories and storytellers do.

We considered several devices before we settled on the one that you'll read below. At first, for example, we imagined the book as a gallery of which we were joint curators, and we considered each chapter as a room or gallery space. However, this only took us so far before the metaphor stopped serving us. So we cast around for further creative inspiration. Somehow, in a way that is as indistinct as the initial tracing lines of a painting, what emerged in the space between us were some characters, alter egos if you like, living in an imaginary future. These became Jas Porter and Imogen Sharp.

Jas came first, unsurprisingly; he was a man of a certain age, like us, who was looking back over his long career in OD and change. Then we imagined he might need someone to act as a counter to his (and inevitably our own) white, middle-aged, male response to the changing world. The idea of a story set between them in the future grew from there, stimulating our creativity, but also in response to a direction of travel we could trace in the world around us: in 2017 as we worked, robots seem to be all the rage. Artificial Intelligence (AI) was in. The media worried about the world of the future with androids replacing humans at work. As we finished the story, the movie *Blade Runner 2049* was hitting the cinemas. It seems we had hit upon the zeitgeist. All thinking is collective thinking.

There was no simple causal relationship between the story and the ideas in the book. It was haphazard and indirect, and for all that messiness, related to the ideas themselves, of the unplanned and the unknowable being experiences to embrace. As we have repeated throughout this book, evolution, like our practice in OD, isn't plannable, but rather it is a sensitive relational interaction with the world around us.

We always intended to draw in a community of people to help us develop our ideas, and the popularity of this AI meme meant that when we advertised an evening event to discuss some of the themes of the book, over 50 people showed up. (Some of their thoughts are incorporated in the commentary that follows the story below.)

It is important to say that whilst we became intent on using this happenstance between the zeitgeist and what we were doing to generate interest in the ideas of the book, we were also mindful that the world we started to create, set 30 to 50 years hence, wasn't about the future – it was about now.

Fredric Jameson observed that science fiction is always about the present, pointing out that:

> even our wildest imaginings are the collages of experience, constructs made up of bits and pieces of the here and now...

> (Jameson, 2005, p.xiii)

It is said that the film writer Woody Allen leaves nuggets of stories on scraps of paper littering his apartment. Sometimes the scraps stay as scraps and sometimes they become the films we watch. So we invited these characters to enact between them a dialogue that stimulated our imagination about the world that OD might face in twenty, thirty, forty, even fifty years' time. It is as if the imaginative process itself helped us to look over the ideas of the book, and consider if they were bold enough to fit, paradoxically, the times we are in now.

> science fiction is a useful tool... due to its ability to make strange whilst
> encouraging critical and reflexive accounts.

> (Smith et al., 2001, p.3)

This is our strange-yet-encouraging account. But having used this imaginal device, we wondered whether it was still worth sharing it with others. We even considered cutting it from the final text of the book. But in some way, that felt dishonest, or even unfair to the characters themselves. It is striking how when you start to create a fiction, the characters develop their own relationships with each other and the wider world. It started to feel like it wasn't our right to kill them off, especially as we had introduced them already to the wider world who had embraced them. They seemed to clarify the ethical and reflexive choices we were trying to elucidate, perhaps better than we did. Ironically perhaps, we had created our own androids who might do us out of a job. So we thought we would share them here, as a kind of denouement, an epilogue that we hope you might find as stimulating to read as we did to write.

Now let us introduce to you the two fictional characters, Jas Porter and Imogen Sharp, who have accompanied us on this OD journey. They live far enough in the future to look back and ask: why did they... ? But not so far that our worlds are totally irreconcilable. With a bit of imagination, we could be there. It was the economist John Maynard Keynes who once said: "The difficulty lies not so much in developing new ideas as in escaping from old ones". This is what Jas and Imogen might prompt us to do. We offer them to you to begin with, as we have done with others, as if they are attending and speaking at a conference, where tradition still has it that short biographical summaries are required. But of course, life is complicated; we have doubts and not all our projects have been a success; so here we have an insight to the characters' shadow sides, something that most of us can relate to but rarely dwell on. It is in finding meaning between the public and private accounts of life that OD may be doing its best work.

Conference bio: Professor Jas Porter

Professor Porter is a world-renowned speaker, teacher and consultant. It would not be over generous to say he is one of the foremost influencers globally in the field of human–android relations. Governments and corporations beat a path to his door. After a number of years working as a consultant in organisation change, for such famous brands as Google, Nautcorp and Artobot, at the forefront of android applications in production, he was invited to join the UN Commission on Human–android Relations and became one of the foremost architects of the UN Convention of 2028. The significance of this work cannot be overstated. As US President Melendez famously said: "The Convention helped us navigate a shift in planetary organisation more profound than the invention of fire, the wheel and the web put together."

But really...

Jas now feels old. He was so optimistic about the work he did, but now fears all it achieved was to loosen the lid of Pandora's box. In his darker moments, he wondered, as Einstein did when pondering his role in unleashing the nuclear genie, if he had not rather have been a watchmaker. He also has a son and now a grandson whose lives are inextricably bound up in the issues about which he theorised at a distance. He finds this deeply troubling. But he is still an optimist. His study and practice of human organisation over many decades had led him to conclude that in the end, life seems to have a way of growing up through the cracks.

Conference bio: Dr Imogen Sharp

Dr Sharp has a unique and pioneering story. One of the first generation of Mixed Genotypes, she was adopted into an international diplomatic family and hence travelled all over the globe from a very early age. She is fluent in over seventeen languages and holds doctorates in Classical Civilisation, Twentieth Century Social Studies and Android Affairs. In 2050 she was elected to the Presidency of the Global New Education Foundation (GNEF), an international learning community she helped to found, which now has over 45 million members. The GNEF prides itself on being a place of harmonious integration of humans and post-humans. She was recently on the cover of *Time* magazine, which featured her work to ensure that GNEF had a voting position on the UN Security Council, with the headline: "Androids storm the citadel".

But really....

Imogen is confused. She is distrustful with being seen as a kind of leader of the MG and android community and is deeply uncomfortable about the story that increasingly pits android rights against human rights. Her studies of the twentieth century have shown her that difference has always been an issue and she sees the tensions being stirred up by certain media outlets and populist politicians as similar in many ways to what happened in the twentieth and early-twenty-first centuries against people of different races, genders and religions. As far as she is concerned, this is about discrimination and fear. She is also slightly estranged from her family of origin, who she feels, despite clearly loving her, still hold her up as somehow different to her natural born brothers and sisters.

When we started to craft the story of our two characters, we had in mind some significant challenges that we knew the world of OD to be avoiding and which it needed to face. These challenges include:

- Increasing levels of automation to the point where androids will be doing many of the jobs currently being done by people
- Rising population numbers, political unrest and ecological stress will increase global tensions and stimulate further major migrations of people
- Personal identities (of race, genotype, gender etc.) will become more complex and these will drive different expectations about the nature of work and careers
- The ethical choices organisations face between human flourishing and efficiency of productive technologies.

Imagining the world of Jas and Imogen helped us ponder how well equipped we in the world of OD practice are to deal with these issues as they affect the organisations and the people in them with whom we work. We tried to imagine what doing OD in the workplace will be like in the face of some of these challenges. It also served as a mirror for our practice today: by exploring a different world we hoped to see ours in different ways, ways that our routines blind us to.

What will the world be like in 2048? How will people live and work? What will their organisations be like? What will be their main preoccupations and how will OD, or its equivalent then, address these? Asking these questions, and responding to them with a story, raises our game by raising our sights. This is reminiscent of C. Wright Mills's book *The Sociological Imagination*; lifting our gaze from what affects us to change our interaction with others as we work into the future (Wright Mills, 1959).

We also wanted to disrupt the idea of a text book – to make it more fun. We hoped it would also show our own faltering artfulness, a yearning and intent to work more imaginatively. It may even give others the permission to be more artful.

In this way of seeing, the context and relevant ideas meld together. This has its problems; how does it translate to your world? All we can do is show our own attempts, drawing on our own context, as a way getting at this contingent nature of the knowledge. It also enables us to look at our current context more critically, with your help. We start our story in 2048.

The bubble – 2048

As he entered the room, the ambient light dimmed. Everything in the University's new bubble suite worked automatically. It unsettled him. A disembodied, androgynous voice spoke.

"Welcome Dr Porter".

"Are you... er... real?" he replied, unable to stop himself.

"Wait a moment", said the voice.

There was a pause. Then a noticeably different, perhaps more recognisably human voice spoke. It was getting harder to discern android from 'real' voices. (Androids had agreed that they weren't offended by the term 'real'; and unlike humans, androids could make a collective agreement and stick to it, without faltering, generally speaking.) Most people, especially the non-android natives born before about 2020, could still tell the difference. Those born later increasingly did not make the distinction – or perhaps were not that interested in it.

"Morning. Anything we can help you with?"

"I wasn't... sure," Jas Porter started haltingly.

"S'okay," said the technician, "They don't have any feelings. Sorry, just my techie humour." He laughed emptily. "I can help you with the bubble this morning."

"But I thought human... people... I thought technicians weren't being used anymore, that it was all done by androids now."

"Well, the system is still being bedded in and there maybe a few glitches. Besides, with some of the... some of the pre-Gendroid generation", (Jas knew he meant 'older') "we like to be on hand in case they get... have problems with the kit."

Jas knew what the technician meant. Some twentieth-century-born people still refused to speak with androids and even campaigned against them. To counter this, students had marched globally for android rights.

"OK. It should all work automatically, but if you need any help touch your ear."

Jas instinctively moved to the interface in his ear, then nodded. "Yes. Ok. Thanks."

As he stepped into the space, a shimmering, silver bubble about ten metres wide appeared to hover in the space around him. He noticed a chair in the centre of the globe, so he sat. He heard a chime and a face appeared on the surface of the sphere, then another, then a third. The first one waved, floating on the silver surface, there was a hiss of static and the one that waved grew larger and moved to the centre in front of Jas. It was like being inside a vast underwater bubble of air, with its surface an iridescent canopy of human faces. The one that was front and centre smiled and said "Hello!" Then abruptly, everything went dark.

"Hello?" Jas was momentarily stunned by the gloom and his finger jabbed his ear.

"Wait a moment," the technician's bored voice came back. "It's crashed. Hold on..."

There was a pause. Then he spoke again.

"Sorry Prof, I'm afraid you have to go out and come back in again."

"What?!"

"Just leave the bubble space, close the door, then turn around and come back in again."

"Oh you're kidding!"

"No... sorry... really, it should all switch off and when you come back in it will reboot."

Jas did what he was told and five minutes later he was back inside the now-functioning sphere. More than twenty faces appeared around its arc. As before, when someone spoke, their face would enlarge and come to the foreground then shrink back as they gave way in the conversation to someone else. If they started a side conversation, their images would merge together on the bubble's silver surface.

A tall androgynous figure appeared in front of him. It was an android avatar, who, Jas now realised, would be hosting the show. For a moment, he panicked. He was unsettled by the appearance of this figure and didn't quite know how he felt about it. As ever, this new world was catching him by surprise. "Welcome everyone. We are delighted to be joined by Professor Jas Porter. As you know, Professor Porter was one of the foremost theorists of organisational development in the 2010s and 2020s, one of the architects of the UN Convention of Global Android–human Relations, and we are privileged to have him join us to participate in the first of this series of bubble-fences entitled 'Who does the work? Android–human relations at work'."

Jas shuffled in his chair, embarrassed by the hagiography.

"But first, we begin with a short holo-show to set the scene, from our sponsor, Artobot Corp."

The Avatar faded to be replaced at the centre of the sphere by a holographic flight across vast sunlit fields of crops alternating with solar farms. A sponsor's jingle rang out and the scene faded to another avatar narrating the various cutaways of micro-automated production lines, robot labs and city-scapes. "In 2028, the United Nations passed the android charter and now, twenty years later, despite some ups and downs, androids are a fully established and cherished part of our global community…"

Jas's thoughts drifted away from the triumphal narration. He looked at the faces around the bubble, intently watching the holoscene that hovered in front of them. He couldn't avoid feeling out of touch with this world, changed out of all recognition from the one that he had inhabited before his own retirement some ten years before. He still wondered why they had asked him to participate in this. He had asked his old friend, who had convened these gatherings, what her reasons were for inviting him. As she had said:

"People are lost, Jas. They feel deeply unnerved. No-one knows what will happen next. People seriously ponder humanity's redundancy."

"But they always have. Even back in F.W. Taylor's time, in the early twentieth century, people thought that machines would take over the workplace. Look at Fritz Lang's movie, *Metropolis*. That was in 1927! It didn't turn out like that!"

"Yes but now it is a major issue. Those countries that don't support a universal basic income, or taxing androids, have got major civil unrest. It's what people fear."

"But what can I do?"

"We hope that people like you, with your reputation, can… calm things down, reassure people. Help us to create some sensible discussion amidst the hysteria. You are someone who seemed to have the ability to make sense of chaos. When we worked together back in the 2020s, you had some insight. You knew how to ask the right questions. I thought you might be able to help."

"I don't know what will happen next. I am not some kind of visionary."

"I know, but you were always such a good… listener. You helped us make sense of it. Make it less fearful."

So it was on this basis that he had agreed to take part, although, right now, as he watched the propaganda in front of him, Jas was having serious doubts.

The holoscene finished and it was time for him to stand up and say something.

As ever, he didn't know quite what he would say until he began.

"I am not going to try to tell you what the future of android–human working relationships will be, because I don't know. I don't know what the future of work will be like, because I don't know. I didn't know back in the 2020s and I don't know now. People say I am some kind of expert about android–human life, but my wife will tell you I don't know how to operate our microwave. What I do know is that ever since the Penrose Equation truly unlocked AI, humanity has struggled with the implications of a mutual intelligence in their midst.

"In one way, this has been a revolution, one vastly more profound than any that have gone on before, even compared to the invention of the World Wide Web. But in other ways, it is just business as usual. It isn't that different to the invention of printing, or the industrial revolution, electricity or indeed the invention of the internet. Each time, the pattern is the same. Everyone thinks they live in the time of the apocalypse. But one thing I do know about people is that we adapt. So the question comes, how do we learn to adapt this time? What we did try and do when we were working on the UN Convention was create a space for dialogue. That's all we did really. It wasn't the answer and it wasn't meant to be. It was the process that mattered – how we went about it, and how we go about it now, how we go about keeping that dialogue going. So, in order that I don't eat my own words about dialogue, I am going to pass over to you now. Let's have a conversation about what it's like in the workplace, right now, and see if we can emerge with some kind of clarity together."

A young, t-shirted face enlarged at the centre of the bubble.

"I am not that interested in the androids and stuff. I think it is bigger than this."

There was a ripple of laughter across the sphere: nothing had seemed bigger than android relations of late. It was what everyone was talking about, everywhere.

"We should care about it," said the t-shirt, "but my organisation, those I work for, I never see. They use an algorithm to make decisions. It's all automated."

"But people are still involved surely?" Jas asked

"I wish they were a bit more. But hardly. They just move on."

"How does that work?"

"If the work changes, the system responds, changes the shape and design, recruits or hires globally. Nobody's hands are dirtied, and people just accept it and move on."

"Do they, though?"

"Well I don't know; it's a seller's market. People know they can get other work elsewhere when they log on to the exchange. So what if their next placement is on another continent? They work virtually anyway."

"It all sounds, very… dispassionate…"

"But it's all in the mix. I'm on my fifteenth placing across four territories in five years. That's what gendroids expect."

Jas noticed that the way this young man spoke (Jas thought he was a man but couldn't be sure) was quite expressionless in some ways. He couldn't be absolutely sure he wasn't an android himself. He wondered about the way that human and android styles of communication seemed to be merging, coalescing and evolving.

"But what about identity, loyalty…?"

"Look, I am a member of a local hub. That's my tribe. And I have all my social hangouts online. They are my buddies. The place I work for… it's just a logon. The universal basic income fills the gaps anyway."

Another face loomed, this time older and more recognisable to Jas, as that of a woman.

"That's all very well, but I work in a government organisation. My experience is that most of us still work in relatively conventional ways, in relatively conventional businesses, using androids only peripherally. We can get carried away with the idea that everyone's world of work has been transformed. Like the web in the 1990s and 2000s – I read about it – nearly everyone has been touched by it, many have found their workplace transformed out of all recognition. New jobs and whole professions have been created, to be sure, but most have muddled through in relatively untransformed, conventional set ups. We still have the same old problems of people alienated from their work, hierarchies, siloes, inefficient working practices, and changes made without taking the views of the employee into consideration. We use androids, yes, but more at the periphery."

One of the faces on the bubble coloured. "I'm sorry. I don't want to intrude… it's just that, whilst we don't mind the term 'real', we do object to the idea of 'using'."

Jas caught on that the person speaking was in fact an android.

"So you are saying that you and your… fellow androids can be offended by that?"

"It isn't a big issue, but some in the a-sense think that being 'used' is a derogatory term. We prefer 'working with'. It isn't that it really bothers us *per se*; we just think it sets the wrong tone. Especially now that we are taxed and supposedly have the same responsibilities and rights at work as h-sense."

Jas noticed the terms 'h-sense' and 'a-sense', which were new to him. He was used to the terms 'a-world' (for android world) and 'h-world' (for human world). But as he thought it through now, perhaps setting androids and humans up as two different worlds may not have been that helpful. He also pondered about what a minefield this was and how all of this was just so damn complicated!

More contributions followed across the bubble. People talked about how radical the changes had been for some and how this was less the case for others. About how the social contract between employers and employees had in some places all but disappeared. Some organisations had gone the other way and there were stories of highly democratic, happy and productive workplaces where people and androids of all colours and shapes seemed to work together (although the cynic in Jas wondered about how much of a gloss was being put on these narratives). In no time at all, the session was winding to a conclusion.

The avatar reappeared. "I think that's about all we have time for today, so I just want to thank you all, and if I may, do some summing up of the key messages we have got from our excellent, lively conversation. I would say that this is about respecting differences, creating dialogue, listening to each other, and being optimistic that the workplace can be an excellent blend of human and android collegiality. It just goes for me to thank Professor Jas Porter on all of our behalves." There was a waving of hands across the bubble and, after more felicitations, the session faded.

As Jas walked away, he admired the intelligence and brightness of younger people. He wondered how he would cope if he had to find a job nowadays. "Thank god I've retired!" he muttered. He thought of his own children who seemed to be getting by despite working in ways that didn't make sense to him. But then he also considered how, in some ways, so little had changed. In the bright lights of the technology, so much in the end came down to people (h- and a- varieties) just listening, respecting and acknowledging each other's differences just like the avatar has said.

Daddy droid – 2028

Twenty years earlier, in 2028, Jas sat on the stage in the conference suite of a large hotel. He listened as the woman at the lectern finished her presentation:

"And so to conclude, I would like to reiterate that current neuro-scientific research shows that consciousness is actually just the brain's illusion of itself. It is as much an electro-chemical process at its root as reproduction or respiration. We have been concerned for years that this consciousness is surely not something so material. We have had that argument ever since Descartes. Surely we are not androids ourselves? This is not a question we have come to recently. After all, Julian de la Mettrie wrote *L'homme Machine* in 1748. But if you look at the processes of the root proteins of the brain, then we can see these are just robots; not simple robots, but robots within robots within robots – complex structures in a highly evolved system that has had billions of years to refine itself. So the current debates about androidity come down in the end to the fact that we are no different to them. In fact, we are they and they are us. Thank you."

The speaker finished and the audience clapped politely, murmuring approval. Jas's mind had drifted nostalgically during the lecture, as it was now prone to do. He remembered faces, names, places and times which seemed so simple, more black and white to him now; but of course, the reality of the 2000s and 2010s was complex. His mind drifted; he would soon be meeting his son again, for the first time in a year. He was over in Europe for a visit and it turned out their paths would cross in Geneva. His son had something to tell him. They were to have lunch together straight after this conference. But now it was his turn to speak. He shook himself from his reverie and began:

"So what I would like to say, to sum up, is that the distinction between androids and humans may be blurred by the so-called scientific evidence, but this doesn't detract from the fundamental proposition that our work in change still comes down to the same things it always has. Contact, relationship, connection, understanding difference and ultimately, dare I say, even love. It comes down to the effectiveness of relationships as well as rational processes. It is an emotive thing, and the skills and capacities that we require to do the work well in any system, be it human–human or android–human or even for that matter android–android, is an emotional experience. We have found that as we blur the distinction, and make androidity more like humanity, this doesn't change anything. We must look to our own prejudices, such as those we used to have about race, age and gender in the last century. It still makes our work in change the same – a political, relationship-based craft, where we must look reflexively to ourselves as the instrument of change, be vulnerable in our not knowing, as we work with complexity, with all the artful and ethical challenges that this brings. There may be no distinctions anymore between us and our humanoid cousins, but that doesn't actually change *change*. It doesn't answer the quest for our soul. Thank you."

Later, he sat opposite his son Mike on a terrace overlooking the lake.

"It is good to see you."

"You too, Dad. Great lecture." He noticed his son seemed nervous, not quite looking him in the eyes.

"Thanks. It was good of you to come. I know these things are a bit dull. I wish it could have been more interactive, more of a dialogue. But the UN is still stuck in the dark ages when it comes to this type of thing. It's all so formal."

His son shook his head. "It was fine. Interesting. Relevant even."

"Why, thank you. Some of what the old man has to say may still be useful to you youngsters you mean?"

"No sorry, I meant... It may be relevant to what we are going to talk about. Right now."

"Oh ok." Jas felt a tightening in his stomach.

His son paused, looked away and then down. He shuffled nervously and toyed with his napkin.

"It is great that we ended up being here at the same time," Jas ventured.

"Yes."

"You are looking well."

"I am well. I'm happy." Mike finally looked squarely at him. Fleetingly, Jas felt it as a challenge.

"That's good. How long since we last saw each other?"

"About a year. I was back home, just before Eelin and I left for China."

"Yes that's right. And how is that going?"

"Well. It's going well. The new Centre is doing some great work. You should come and see it. I would love to show you around."

"I don't go to China very much anymore."

"No."

"But you are back in Europe now. For how long?"

"The andro-genetics conference starts here tomorrow, goes on to the end of the week. Then I go back via London as I wanted to see you and Mum. There is... some news."

A waiter, clattering down their cups of coffee, interrupted the moment.

"You said there was some news?", Jas started, as soon as the waiter was beyond earshot.

"Yes, I have some news." Mike said firmly.

"That sounds... interesting."

Mike half smiled. "'Interesting'. One of your favourite words."

"OK, it sounds ominous actually."

"No it's fine. It is just that... The good news is... I don't know how to say this without just blurting it out. You are going to be grandparents."

Jas gasped and then beamed. He clapped his hands together as he always did when he was overcome with emotion or laughter.

"That's fantastic! I'm delighted. Your mother will be thrilled."

"Will she though?" Mike looked across the water with a frown.

"Of course! Why not? Mikey that's great news!"

"Well, there's a... bit of a catch."

"How can there be a catch? Is there something up with you and Eelin?"

"No, no, we are just fine. But. Look: Eelin isn't the mother."

"Oh." Jas half knew what it was that Mike was about to say. He knew the work that Mike and his partner Eelin were involved in and he had also heard about the programme from others. After all, it wasn't a coincidence that Mike got into this line of work, growing up as he did in the shadow of his father's work on the Convention. The work of the Andro-Genetics Centre where Mike worked was highly reputed, yet controversial. Jas was conflicted about it. Part of him was excited by the possibilities, but in his gut sat a half-acknowledged flutter of doubt, a semi-conscious qualm.

"Don't get me wrong. It isn't an affair or love triangle or anything. It is that... there isn't a mother as such. I mean she will be... giving birth to the child, but. Oh this is a bit hard..."

"Mike, I think I understand," said Jas, trying to stay matter of fact. Mike seemed oblivious as children are to their parents' attempts to make life easier for them.

"Eelin and I, you know we both work at the Centre. And they were looking for volunteer couples for the new A–H programme. Android v4.0."

"The programme where Advanced Android Human Hybrids are being mooted.

Mike was clearly irritated by his father's lack of awareness.

"We... don't like the term hybrids. We think it is offensive. We prefer Mixed Genotypes. MGs."

"Ah. Sorry."

"So... Eelin and I volunteered for the programme. We are parenting in the first group of MGs. Eelin is the surrogate and I provided the genetic material along with others in the group."

"So. Our first grandchild... will be... ?"

"Technically you are one of six grandparents. The child in question... he will be three-quarters human, one-quarter android."

"It's a boy?"

"Yes. The thinking is that this MG world is complex enough without blurring gender distinctions at this stage. Although that will come for sure."

"I'm sure..." Jas tried to sound enthusiastic.

"You predicted it, in your work with the Convention."

"Yes... I... I know I did."

Mike recovered his enthusiasm.

"Yes, it is a unique programme. And we are *so* excited to be amongst the first. And we are getting guaranteed state support, full education rights, medicare, and to be part of a pioneering study the child will be so well looked after and Eelin and I are really, like, *psyched* about this..." He slowed to a halt as he noticed the expression on his father's face. "I *knew* you would find this hard..."

Jas sighed.

"I am not finding it hard. I am delighted. OK maybe it is a bit hard. It just, takes a little... getting used to, that's all."

"Why should *you* find it hard, of all people!? Someone who was just, in there," (He pointed towards the conference call that Jas had just left), "banging on about how nothing really changes. It's all about relationships. There are no distinctions anymore. The work of change doesn't change yada, yada..."

"Mike, give me a chance. Please. It is as if you were just waiting for me to trip up. Listen, my grandfather would have been scandalised by someone from our family marrying a non-Jew, or someone outside the shtetl. Now you wonder why I may find this a little challenging? But I am really happy, happy for you both. For me, us. I really am. But the reality... is still confronting. I can't deny that. It will take a little... time to adjust. Even, as you say, for me. Someone who should know better."

* * * *

A year later, Jas and his wife stood in the airport arrival hall, waiting for Mike, Eelin and baby to walk through the gate. Jas felt nauseous with anticipation.

How would it be? He knew all the theory, all the thinking that had brought him to this moment of change, all the art he had expressed in supporting this moment, yet when confronted with it himself, an ugly discomfort had surfaced in him that he had been wrestling with for the past year. The irony of someone who stood on platforms, extolling openness to the kind of future so many were resisting, pontificating on how the fundamentals of social engagement will never change...

Finally, the doors swung open and there was his son, smiling and holding a small bundle: the baby, dressed in a white babygro and slung inside a pouch. Eelin alongside him looking happy, pushing a bag cart. In that awkward moment of catching each other's eyes but before they could speak, Jas could feel... what was it? It was an ancestral weight fall away.

They came together with noises of greeting, kisses and hugs, and Mike said:

"Mum, Dad, this is Jo."

Jas looked into the baby's eyes and it cooed. And from that moment, everything fell away for Jas. Every single bit of knowing, except one, which was love.

Ghost boats – 2030

2030. He watched the boats in the harbour gently swing downwind on their anchors. Last night, jetlagged, unable to sleep, he had got out of bed and padded down to the small beach in front of the hotel. Meaning only to dip his toes in the warm ocean, an impulse had taken over and he found himself pajama-less, naked, lying on his back in the gentle shallows of the South China Sea, watching the stars. A meteorite flashed across the corner of his eye. He gaped at the rushing water and the vast night sky. Momentarily becalmed, he forgot who he was and why he was here.

Now, some 10 hours later, he sat in front of his client's desk in the corner office on the forty-seventh floor. The sea glinted through steamy tropical air. He felt a familiar, unreal, suspended, underwater sensation brought on by his body having been forced across time. This, combined with being a foreigner in Asia, usually gave him a feeling of being at some disadvantage in encounters like this one. The client had momentarily welcomed him into the office then disappeared, apologising, saying there was just something urgent she had to do. She reappeared some ten minutes later. He thought that was odd.

As he waited, his mind chewed over what he had been recently reading. On the flight over, he had been nostalgically reviewing some of their old writings and blogs. Officially retired, he was unable to give up working. He still couldn't resist being wanted, especially when it involved first-class travel. One particular blog had caught his eye, which, he mused, they had written over a quarter of a century before:

> Like all beliefs, I have one that could probably do with being shaken up. What has always been required for deep learning to occur is ongoing, deep and trusting contact between the learner and their human environment of learning. The best courses I've even been on, or facilitated, have always been the best because of the level of contact created as a learning community, not just between teacher and learner, but more often between learner and fellow learner. Whatever it has been, from learning Hebrew on Kibbutz between picking cotton in Israel when I was 19, to being taught to ride a motorbike by some fat bloke in leathers called Smithy, to deep practice in facilitation or emotional intelligence taught beneath heartbreakingly beautiful sunsets by humble, solid teachers with incalculable presence; what strikes me now about all of these is that the stimulus to absorb was in the sensual detail of connection between me and that environment, usually in the human aspects of that environment (i.e. other people). It is this sensuality that is missing from me if we try to replicate these communities solely in a virtual environment."

These words struck him as deeply ironic, considering his reason for being here today. Then the client reappeared.

"So Dr Porter, we are delighted that you have come to Singapore to advise us again. How long has it been since you were last here?"

"It must have been ten years ago, around the time we were working on the Convention." Jas couldn't help mentioning the work that had been the summit of his career and become his leitmotiv, but about which he was now increasingly uncomfortable. When he caught himself, he was embarrassed by it.

"That's right, and you were helping us with the fleet at that time?"

"Yes I was, and of course Singapore was at the centre of Android v2.0 at that time."

"Ah yes, a brave and proud time in our history. It was before my time, or course." That was an understatement. This young woman couldn't be more than twenty, yet here she was occupying a corner office in the headquarters of one of the largest shipping fleets in the world. He mused that she wouldn't have been a teenager yet when they were working out the first fundamental codes of android–human relationships.

"Nautcorp was at the centre of it. It was vital that you role-modelled a commitment to maintaining the dignity of human work at a time when many global corporations were wondering if they could do away with people altogether.

"Yes, by that time the algorithmic movement had worked out that we could totally automate our fleet".

"*Near*-totally automate," Jas stressed.

"Yes. Quite right. Safety was always the concern, although we know that human presence on ships actually makes things less safe. But people weren't happy to make that call back then. And the dignity of human labour; that was written into our constitution."

Jas noticed the 'was'. A distant alarm rang in his mind.

"So Nautcorp's commitment became a keystone project. We worked out how people could work with androids and how this shifted the dynamics of human–human working relationships as well. Doing so for sailors on long-distance voyages was a great testing ground for this. It was like what Will Shutz did with sailors on nuclear submarines in the 1950s, when he developed FIRO."

"FIRO?"

"FIRO – Fundamental Interpersonal Relations Orientation. It was a tool we used to use to help teams work together. Way back when."

"Ah. Back in the days when only people made up teams?"

"Yes, that's right." Jas shifted in his chair and felt all of his years. Some more words from that blog came to him:

> I thought it was my failure, my lack of hip, up-to-the-minute social learning literacy that meant I wasn't cool enough to get with the online, virtual plan... "Hang on", I said, giving myself a stiff talking to, "I have been doing this a long time. I know that the skills of action learning facilitation are hard earned, and about self-awareness, skilful feedback and engagement. This is how in fact you do the real job of social learning; moving from the facilitator/teacher as the one who has the (content-based) answer to creating a genuine social space for conversational, practical learning, across an engaged and intimate group."

Engagement and intimacy? They had found out, of course that it was possible for humans and machines to become intimate, to engage, at least in some simulacrum of intimacy. They had pondered long and hard whether the illusion of intimacy was as good as the real thing, but all that debate had done was question whether such a thing had ever existed in the first place.

The client shifted in her seat and he noticed an awkward mirroring of his own movements. For the first time, he wondered for a moment if this was just a cross-cultural, intergenerational tension, a young Asian woman with a European man from a different age, old enough to be her grandfather. Or was it something else? A moment before, he had been marvelling at how, in this day and age, a young woman could have done so well in scaling the corporate ladder. That had struck him as great progress. Now though, he was wondering if she had disappeared for ten minutes to change her power pack. He knew that v3.0 could be remarkably human-like.

"Dr Porter, let's move on to why we are here today. Shall we do that?"

"Yes that would be great."

"I will come straight to the point. Over the last ten years, our own position on the Convention has... shifted. We have been doing our own culture surveys, profiling our workforce, crunching the data of social surveys and we found that some of the principles of the Convention, that we built into our own constitution... they have become... increasingly... irrelevant."

"Ah. I see."

"It seems that the issues that really concerned people... Well, they seem to have gotten over them. Especially since Android v3.0. The upgrade has meant people don't even blur the distinction anymore. At least not in some of our key territories. Asia, Russian Empire, most of the American States. So we would like your help to... ease a further transition."

"A transition?" Jas knew what was coming. He had long suspected it would lead this way. And then it came.

"We would like to fully automate now. We have a fleet of over 500 ships and we want to remove human crew from them all."

"This is a very big step. Nautcorp's role in the Constitution was key." The thought of those 500 boats ploughing the ocean sent a slight shiver through him. No human voices. Ghost boats.

"Believe me, Dr Porter, we have done our research. People really don't care to make the distinction anymore. And safety isn't now perceived as an issue. People have just got used to the idea of androidity. Your work has been a huge success."

"So what do you need from me? You can just go ahead and do it. Why do you need any help. My skills are about the interface between people and androids."

"That interface has shifted again. That's how we see it anyway. We are not entirely without concern for how this looks. We know it represents a big step, especially considering the role that Nautcorp played in the Convention. The politics of this are... sensitive. It is a symbolic step more than anything else because we have slowly been removing human involvement as v3.0 has been coming in. We thought you could be... figural... in the campaign."

"Ah. So you want me to give it my pubic blessing?"

In his head the thought made him shudder: basically, they need me to help them make it look good. He could feel himself getting warm and he tried hard to maintain his composure.

"That's not quite all of it. But yes, in a nutshell. There is some work to be done; some real work. We have stakeholders, customers; the few remaining human staff who we need to support in this transition to full automation. Also the brand presidents are an increasingly powerful force and we have to keep them on board. We have some events and a programme of work schedule as we make the transition and we thought you could facilitate this work with us. It wouldn't take up too much of your time. We would ensure you had a group of our people to work with and you could do as much or as little of the actual face-to-face work as you liked. And of course, we would pay you. You could name your fee."

That night, still unable to sleep, Jas lay again in the warm ocean, looking up at the stars. He was comforted only by the thought he was going home tomorrow. The conversation with the client sat uneasily with him. Could he be part of this brave new world? How could he justify being the one that helped to turn out the light on another whole human industry? Was it a betrayal of his work on the Convention, which had seemed to safeguard a harmonious working relationship between people and androids? Or was it just another shift in the sands between humans and their technological progeny? Would he see himself as a Luddite, or a saboteur, resisting progress or, like Taylor or Lewin, supporting a new relationship, a new conversation between people and what they defined as their work? After all, like life between the cracks in a pavement, whenever it seemed human work was finished, whole new vocations sprang into life, unpredicted by the generations before. But there was always a cost: those who felt left behind, unable to move quickly enough, who get run over by the change juggernaut. Was he one of them? The words they had written in that blog so long ago seemed more prescient now than they could ever have imagined.

A predictable future? – 2035

Stafford Beer was a cyberneticist of the 1960s who thought that the solutions to all the world's problems were to be found through central planning informed by sophisticated computing. One of his biggest clients was Salvador Allende, the Marxist President of Chile. His computers told him how to plan, monitor and adjust the economy. Any planned system, though, cannot cope with unplanned events or those that lie outside of the system. In Allende's case, this unforeseen force came in the form of its powerful neighbour to the north and its support for a fascist revolution in Chile that brought death to Allende.

Monocultures are also a product of the central-planning mindset. Prosperity and efficiency are the goal of the monoculture. German forestry, with line after line of spruce, the wheat fields of the US in the early twentieth century and the potato famine in Ireland in the mid-nineteenth century were all monocultures and all ultimately led to the death and displacement of millions.

All of these have one thing in common: good intentions from the centre; a paternalism that leads of its own destruction. There are a number of reasons for this: hubris, a lack of knowledge of local conditions, a myth that with a large enough computer, complexity can be tamed. Sometimes it is blind faith that a great plan only needs faithful execution. There is a consistent theme: whatever our technological ability, hope for a better future beguiles us into failing to imagine a darker side.

In 2030, they had promised a whole new society. Jas had always been a sceptic. But their logic was compelling. Now it was possible, they argued, to plan and nudge human behaviour towards predictability. It was all about 'objective data and measurement'. In the late 2010s and early 2020s, following a rise of populism and crumbling of power in the supra-national institutions like the EU and the UN, governments offered utopian visions based on hyper-neoliberalism, populism and 'big data'. Everything was measureable and doable now, they argued. AI was so sophisticated that it was able to master the required complexity. It was just a matter of predicting the patterns. In 2030, countries like Russia, the US, Turkey, China, planned and started to build vast highly automated mega-cities, with mind boggling speed. Populations were offered 'stakeholder shares' that they could repay over their own and their children's lifetimes. It was all done from the top down. What Jas objected to most was that dissenting voices were ignored or, worse still, ostracised and ridiculed. It was a massive monoculture of thinking. He had always been a fan of diversity, in both being and thinking. Monocultures of the mind are dangerous of course. But conformism was the order of the day. Get with the plan.

It was all supposed to be 'scientific', with no margin for human error. Big data was crunched using massive data centres and highly complex algorithms. Jas could see that what they were measuring was highly subjective. People were basically rewarded for agreeing with the official line, be it corporate, governmental or both. Then this data was presented back to them as 'objective truth'.

He always wondered if he could have done more to prevent what happened. Of course, he knew he was only a small cog in a much larger mechanism, but he had been there advising the government at the time when hyper neoliberalism had reached its apotheosis, albeit that he had been part of the group that was trying to challenge the extreme audit culture. This, they later realised, had driven policies that had directly lead to the mega crash.

"We now have the big data that can help us plan objectively for the kind of social engineering we need. The time of uncertainty has passed." So said the big-data guy at a UN meeting to which Jas had been invited.

"I want to challenge that," he had said. "There are always factors we can't anticipate. What you are measuring is subjective. You incentivise people to agree with you, so they can get a higher approval rating on social media and more likelihood of placement in the new projects."

It was as if he hadn't spoken. "But we now have the capacity to predict to a higher level of complexity than suggested by the 10 billion people on the planet," the data guy had countered. "These policies will surely work because we have mapped them to a greater degree than is humanely possible to act, in any combinations. Our android friends have given us the certainty we have never before enjoyed."

The big-data guy said *humanely* possible rather than *humanly* possible. Jas had noticed the Freudian slip. What he and his friends had failed to recognise was that it would be androids who would drive the cyber crash that collapsed the world financial system by erasing all the data in one instant. They did it with good intentions, of course – or at least the good intentions of their programmers. But nevertheless, there we all were on that fine June day in 2035, waking up to a world where simply nothing worked. All the data had gone. Apart from the androids themselves, of course; their operating systems had been designed to work independently as well as collectively. It had taken a long debate to make that happen. Ultimately, the argument was won by those who believed that a mix of both independent and collective logics in androids would most closely mirror human thinking – luckily for us all. Without them, we would never have been able to piece any of it back together again. But meanwhile, planes had crashed, nuclear plants had gone into near meltdown, ships had wandered aimlessly around the oceans without data links – and the vast new hyper cities planned through the 'inexorable algorithms of big data' became sites of massive civil unrest, or had simply been abandoned, as people streamed out into the countryside. By 2040, most of these mega cities were being reclaimed by the forests and savannahs they had temporarily displaced.

And then the post-neoliberal movement had begun what Jas considered the vast overreaction of populist hyper-localism. Another round of expert bashing and anarchic romanticism. People refuted all large-scale systems, anything smacking of expertism was rejected. A global throwing out of babies and bathwater was pursued.

Jas and his own community weren't too badly affected, of course. But it niggled him daily – could he have spoken up more loudly for what he now knew to be true, but back then was only a belief that flickered in the howling wind of ardent opposition? Namely that the neoliberal reaction to the credit crunch of years before, in the late 2000s – which was to become even more staunch in the audit culture, more strident in the setting of targets and measuring impact 'objectively' using big data that now had, supposedly, the computing power to iron out any margins of error – was just a fallacy? That measurement and evaluation were always a subjective, contingent and unpredictable craft? And it always depended on who was looking? How ironic was it that the very machines that promised an error-free future had, in their intent to put that into practice, caused the very meltdown they had said was now impossible?

But now, Jas was faced daily with the protestations of young students who had, as young people do, reacted in the extreme to what they saw as any attempt to predict, to plan, to create universal systems, and clung to a localist romanticism that Jas suspected would only lead to another disaster marking the victory of ideology over reason.

Imogen and the book – 2048

Imogen opened the old book. She wasn't used to dealing with something made of paper that had actual pages. Her hands fumbled, the paper seemed so rough to the touch. Normally she was so dextrous, when flicking through the windows on a tablet or waving though a sky board. But this thing was tricky. She tried flicking but found that she kept skipping and missing out pages. So she held the back of the book in one hand and turned each page independently from the top. That seemed to work better.

She started to read the chapter:

> Organisation development is a planned and emergent set of undertakings, designed to create greater clarity and focus around an organisation's strategy, culture and leadership. It has many different manifestations, proposed by different people, who sit on a continuum from those who see it as a highly structured plan of activities to those that see it as about local and relational dialogue, where the practitioners themselves is as open to change and being changed as the system they are supporting. The view of this author is that the latter is a more sustainable and effective approach in the long run...

Imogen continued to read and she found herself agreeing with much of what the author had said.

She found herself auditing the sentences as she read, considering their relevance to today's world. There were some parts that seemed very archaic. Of course, there was no mention of androids or hybrids and the world seemed, from the way things were laid out, like a more orderly place. From what the author was saying, people tended to work in one place, with one employer, who they might stay with for some length of time. This was unlike the way people moved around now, sometimes on a daily basis, and how they identified less with the organisation that commissioned them (who they ultimately worked for) than the agency they worked through or the brand tribe to which they were signed up.

The case studies also seemed very archaic. She realised as she read that there were whole industries at the time that the book was written that no longer existed. (She found that if she looked at one of the first pages of the book, it seemed to give a date of publication, which was 2002.) She wondered what 'accountants' did, and nursing seemed to have been a very different profession then. Nurses seemed to work much longer, harder hours, and they seemed to be tied to conducting much more hands-on and physical support to patients, without the remote operator and android-administered medicine that prevailed today.

"So on the one hand," she said to her friend Tam later, "the world of work seems utterly unrecognisable to today."

"Yes, I guess so. What you showed me read like history", said Tam.

"But on the other hand, there was much that seemed similar."

"Like what?"

"For one thing, people seemed to get drawn into conflicts as much then as they do now, and to try to rely on processes to sort them out, when a good conversation would work better. Like when we set up the research group and no-one could agree what the purpose was. Everyone argued and no-one listened."

"Yes, I see that. My brand leader is useless at sorting out arguments – which is why we all compete to get time with her. She never confronts anything."

"And also what seems to give people a sense of satisfaction doesn't seem to have changed very much."

"Howso?"

"There was this one story of a nurse in this crazy world that seemed to be going on around her, in something called an 'Emergency Ward'. It was a place that people ran to if they were hurt."

"There were no remote booths?"

"No. Nothing like that. So, some people had been hurt in a car accident. They used to drive themselves back then and had tons of accidents. Can you imagine?! Anyway, the mother of this poor kid who was critically ill was outside and she was disturbed, and the nurse decided – even though she was maxed out and there was lots of other stuff to do – to sit with the mother for a bit. And later the mother thanked her so much for staying with her. And she said that it was doing that, and being recognised for it, that had felt like the most important work she had done. I mean, you can relate to that story, right?"

"Yes I can," said Tam.

Walk round the lake – 2048

When he first met Imogen, the image of Rosie the Riveter came to mind. The picture, from the 1940s, that had been a feminist icon in his younger days, was actually made to encourage Americans to buy war bonds so they could support Rosie and women like her to build bombers, which then dropped bombs on German and Japanese cities. This always struck Jas as deeply ironic: ordinary women being empowered through the building of instruments of destruction of others. But like Rosie, Imogen was not someone to mess with.

He could see another parallel: Rosie's generation represented the early 'cyborgs', as Donna Haraway had called them. Technologically enhanced and empowered, they were a new breed, a new species perhaps. Eric Trist had talked some time ago about 'socio technical systems'. (Was that in the 1930s, over a century ago? Jas couldn't believe it.) Technology worked alongside and inside human relationships. Increasingly, technology has been integrated inside the human. From stones to break open oyster shells, sticks to dig up termites and logs used as crutches to eyeglasses, hearing aids, pace-makers, artificial limbs, artificial organs and finally the enhanced neo-cortex of Android v2.0. How were android–human hybrids any different? Weren't they merely part of an evolutionary process centuries old? Donna Haraway had written 'A Cyborg Manifesto' in 1984. The idea that people and machines were emerging into some kind of unpredictable singularity had been sitting with Jas all his life, even way back when he was first taught about what they used to call 'OD'.

He was excited to meet her and of course flattered that she wanted to talk about work he had done years ago, that even he had forgotten about. Yet confronted with Imogen in the flesh, as it were, he couldn't help feeling unsettled again. As he always had. It was like his own father had been with his gay brother – wanting so much to be normal about it, but failing at some deep, limbic level. He was shamefacedly caught in the gap between his espoused and his lived values.

What did Imogen think of Jas? She had heard a lot about him, of course: his reputation, his leading-edge work in android–human relations some two decades before. But when she met him, she couldn't help feeling disappointed. He seemed deflated somehow. He was tired, although putting a brave face on it. Of course he was old; in his eighties. But that wasn't an excuse anymore. People were now living regularly into their hundreds. It was being predicted that an android born now might live two centuries. His professed values, of diversity, openness to change and innovation, what he wrote about, the possibilities of measuring impact in local, timely and specific ways, the craft-like nature of strategy building – it all spoke to her more loudly of hope than he did in person. He seemed wary, as if she was about to take something from him that he was guarding from view.

And now here he was, confronted by a 'real' cyborg (as if Rosie hadn't been real enough). Imogen was what his grandson was. A hybrid person, an MG (mixed genotype) enhanced by the technology that was now available, in the same way that Rosie had been by the rivet gun she found on the factory floor. What was the difference? Imogen's enhancements were built in at the factory. "I am 33 per cent android" she proudly declared as they walked around the Lake. She hoped he would be overjoyed, fascinated but instead he was nervous as if he didn't quite know what to say.

"Yes of course, I have met many hybrids, sorry..." he stuttered.

"Don't worry", she said. She was being kind, although she found his hesitation increasingly galling.

"I mean MGs. They are normal to me. I mean... you are."

"It's OK", she said, then with a bit more edge: "We aren't programmed you know. We respond... normally."

Imogen reflected on her experience of him. She didn't feel like he was treating her normally. She decided to change the subject.

"I wanted to discuss the history that lead up to the treaty."

"Yes, as you said in your message."

"When you were first working in the field. I am interested for my own research."

"Yes, you asked about OD, as we called it."

"That's right. I wondered about the link between the early thinkers and the hyper-localism now. There seems to be a match. An overlap in the thinking."

"You see, when I first started in the field of OD, there were many different styles and approaches, some more formal and some more relationship-focussed, or 'dialogic'. I preferred the latter."

"Working things out through relationship..."

"Yes that's right. But things were different then."

"How so?"

"Well, back then it was only people."

"How is that different to now?"

"I'm sorry."

"No, really."

"I've hurt your feelings."

"It's fine."

"Actually," he sighed, "it reminds me that we used to struggle with people from different backgrounds back then too. We used to trip over our words, thinking of the... correct thing to say."

"Exactly. So the basic challenge of dealing with difference and coming to understand each other through dialogue – how has it changed? It just seems to me that it hasn't. And also how we all need to look at our own biases in order to understand what impact we have on the world. It's the same."

"And something else hasn't changed."

"An old fool learning from youth."

Imogen smiled, just like Rosie in the picture postcard Jas used to have on his office wall.

Endgame? – 2049

The Dean was standing by the window as Jas came into the office. The sun shone through the stained glass.

"I'm afraid it is time to have that conversation."

"Which conversation is that?"

"It's the one where I say I am going to be making a grateful speech about your long and illustrious career with the University over a glass of wine in the Great Hall."

Jas expected to feel a panic. He knew he was avoiding final retirement. His link to the University was a vital one with his past, and it was about to be broken. He wondered when he would feel his feet turn to puddles and a cold shard in his stomach. But instead he just felt calm. Relieved.

"It is a bit ironic to hear that my job is finally going to an android."

"Well now these learning protocols are very sophisticated now. We are restructuring our whole learning and teaching model. Universities are very changed places since we started out."

But Jas knew that the University had been in trouble for a while. It was increasingly irrelevant to the world, and found it harder and harder to attract students and research grants. It was being bypassed by entrepreneurial social systems that were far more adaptable. Later, as he was walking off the campus, Jas bumped into Imogen.

"Good to see you again," she said.

"You too."

"How is it going?"

"I think I just lost my job. Not that I was clear that I really had one, in the strict sense, anymore."

"Who does?"

"Yes, that's right."

"It's good timing really."

"Howso?"

"I'd been meaning to ask you to help us with a project. We need a bit of mentoring. And a figurehead."

"You want to stick me on the front of a ship?"

"Pardon?"

Once again, Jas realised he wasn't funny anymore.

"Never mind."

"Ok. As I say, I'd like to ask you if you'd be interested."

"Well, go ahead. Ask."

"I am. It was a figure of speech."

Again, he found himself tripped up by his own failure to see how human Imogen was.

"My innovation group has decided to leave the University and create our own network-based learning centre. It has created a lot of interest already. We have 400,000 subscribers."

"Wow. How long has that taken you?"

"It's taken a bit of time actually, because we have been doing it carefully, relationally, as you would say. Almost two days. It's a niche channel. And as I said, we'd like a mentor and someone who can help us build the team. We were wondering if you would do that for us?"

Jas smiled. He walked to the rapid transit stop with a spring in his step. Things had changed, yet in some ways, they hadn't.

Looking back – 2058

It had been five years since the last organisation ceased to exist. People were now working for themselves, coming together with others when the need arose, to achieve a paid-for task. People competed with androids and therefore had to stress their unique and unprogrammable qualities. A form of Aldous Huxley's brave new world had become a reality, or at least the worker classifications of Alpha, Beta and Epsilons. Alphas were at the top of the tree, the creatives, artists, actors; they were the ones hardest to replicate. Dentists, doctors and lawyers, the once-comfortable elite, were in keen competition with the ultra-androids. For these groups, a new form of creative professional had emerged, the personal brand president or PBP (the terms 'director' and 'manager' had long since fallen into disrepute). Their task was to develop a brand of the client – each individual was an autonomous competitive agent and providing them with a clear-blue-water differentiation was a lucrative enterprise. It also reflected the deep anxiety of maintaining status as an Alpha or Beta. Those that wavered soon found themselves and their work commoditised with the remaining 80 per cent of the workforce. Instead of relying on PBPs to promote their brand, they relied on the skeleton government's LDS or Labour Distribution Scheme, a minimum wage safety net pitching person against the statutory definition of HFE (higher functional end) androids.

Despite pervasive anxiety, everyone was cheerful. Or at least that is how they related to each other. It was a fragile shell maintained by the legal (and, since last year, encouraged) consumption of opiates. But there were stirrings. Some underground groups campaigned across the virtual space, against androidisation of the workplace. Governments growing uncomfortable and pressurised by the discontent. Populist demagogues added to the febrile atmosphere, and the government of the Federated Union of America (made up of what had been the USA, Canada and south American nations including Brazil and Argentina) was promising a referendum in 2060 on whether it would pull out of the Convention on android rights altogether. In that territory, androids had always been denied the vote...

What sense do we make of it all?

The beauty of a story, of course, is that no-one can dictate how to make sense of it, what to draw from it or how to relate to the characters – least of all us, the authors. It is yours now. Jas and Imogen are as much your friends as ours. Consider the story a gift. Like any gift, it can adorn your mantelpiece or get stuffed into the back of your wardrobe. Your choice.

But having offered it to a number of people, we thought it might be good to offer you what *they* made of it. This is partly to encourage you and also because the quality of their thinking was so good, in our view. Our biggest thanks go to a great group of over 50 colleagues and friends who joined us for an evening of lively discussion and debate, having been introduced to Jas and Imogen, in London in September 2017. The quotes below come mostly from them.

The quality of thinking that emerged from this group bears testimony to the proposition that such thought is founded on the quality of our collective imagination. We are reminded of Palaeolithic cave paintings. Their artists must have been stimulated by the stories of the community that gave birth to them. Were they the equivalent of the OD practitioners of their own age?

Jas and Imogen's story inspired much feedback and this, various as it was, clustered around some significant questions. These were:
- Will organisations as we know them, and therefore OD, soon cease to exist?
- What is the ethical stance of our practice in the face of these challenges?
- Is there still a place for strategy in an unknowable future?
- How do we make meaning in the light of this?

The end of organisation?

The story prompted much conjecture about whether organisations might have a future at all. This started with a question about whether such a practice as OD might exist but then evolved into wondering whether organisations themselves might have a future and that, even if OD isn't called 'OD', perhaps some relational practice would still have a role to play. Maybe it would become everybody's responsibility. In this sense, perhaps the practice we might call 'OD' would come 'into the open', becoming a way of being that everyone might own and benefit from. Some illustrative quotes:
- "I love the idea of OD in the open."
- "Perhaps we are looking at a system without formal management – or at least one that is about a constant state of change."
- "At first, we thought 'OD has ceased to exist', then we sort of crossed

that out. It's just a way of being."
- "What if in 2048 we didn't have management layers in organisations; what if they were completely self-organising? So then the way change and OD works would be entirely different. But still necessary."

How do the ethics of our practice need to develop?

We think that the ethics of OD practice are generally overlooked and we are pleased that people took Jas and Imogen's story as an invitation to consider much more central ethical questions and concerns about OD practice, prompted by the challenge that technology might pose us. People questioned whether the 'post-human' Imogen would have separated public and private voices (for example, in her conference biography) as we all do. After all, this very separation of public and private selves is the ground on which OD stands – think of Schein's classic iceberg model which enshrines that proposition. The notion of public and private selves is already being challenged, of course. Think of how quickly people in the public gaze have their foibles exposed in a social-networking age. Does this in fact encourage us to improve our ethical standards, because there is no hiding place from scrutiny? Perhaps when the science fiction writer Isaac Asimov came up with his Three Laws of Robotics in the 1940s, he was actually talking about how all of us, humans and non-humans alike, should act for the sake of minimising harm to others.* They are laws for all of us. Perhaps the irony of a digital age is it might be prompting us to be better humans.

The other ethical choices people dwelt on concerned how wealth is created and shared. Is it built on the backs of slaves (even post-human ones), as has historically been the case? Can we allow a massive underclass of underemployed humans to continue to grow? These are not just choices we will face, but ones that we are already facing. And OD has a role in challenging these realties. As people said:
- "Perhaps the robots or the androids will end up creating a different understanding of ethics than we actually currently have."
- "A system which works as if all is in the public domain is challenging, but it does suggest that the behaviour of leaders could be forced to improve."
- "Will post-humans force us to be less 'human' in this way or encourage us to be more congruent?"

---

* Asimov's Three Laws of Robotics, which he first codified in 1942 and were made famous by his short-story collection *I, Robot* in 1950, state that:
- A robot may not injure a human being or, through inaction, allow a human being to come to harm.
- A robot must obey orders given it by human beings except where such orders would conflict with the First Law.
- A robot must protect its own existence as long as such protection does not conflict with the First or Second Law.

- "I choose not to have a master–slave relationship."
- "Reflexivity is as an ethical choice."
- "Either we can diminish to the cheapest and most efficient way or we can consider people as part of our product."

Whither strategy?

At the root of most business-school teaching is a faith in the axiom of strategy. Perhaps we too fell into the trap of believing this truth (see Chapter 5) albeit by thinking of strategy as a 'craft', which we dressed up in the clothes of emergence. But people who became acquainted with Jas and Imogen really enjoyed playing with the thought that strategy might be an idea that has had its day. It is based on the realisation that implicit in strategy is a notion that we can't plan our way forward anymore (could we ever?) and that the best we can do is replace it with imagination, even though that is also always based more on what we know now than what we can know about the unpredictable future. Ultimately, it seems that people are genuinely tired of the myth of strategic planning. What would it be to let go of the ever-receding future and just *be*, here and now? Could we dream of running an organisation on this basis? This thinking challenged us greatly and we love it. We think the quotes below exemplify this yearning:

- "Will strategy still be a useful thing in 2048?"
- "If you plan for a particular model of the future, it's almost bound to be wrong."
- "We imagine a future based on current knowledge."
- "Even imagination probably won't get you to where it says it's driving you towards, but it will get you somewhere."
- "Strategy should be 'imagining optimistically'."
- "Imagining is NOT knowing. Or even pretending to know, like strategy."

Our job endures: we are the makers of meaning, the dreamers of dreams...

Throughout our discussions with others, and as the story of Jas and Imogen has evolved, we have been struck by a persistent thought that the world is becoming ever more reliant on relationships, as an ethical position rather than a truth, and that our role in OD might become more required than ever, even if the name of what we do changes. In other words, how could digital thinking drive the possibility of more humanity? Whether we call ourselves OD practitioners or Mercurians, whether we are the cave painters of 30,000 years ago or the personal brand presidents of the 2060s, all of us are helping people make sense of their lives and work through storytelling. And this role may be needed more than ever:

- "We are crafting the future by imagining."
- "Can we put the human back in the story?"

- "Create meaning, support a sense of community wherever it is."
- "Humans are humans, it's just we have got different scenarios and technologies."
- "The fundamentals stay the same."

We are aware that our quoted discussions amount to a very tentative piece of research; it would be wrong to infer too much from this. But in OD there is a diagnostic practice we call the 'as if' principle. That is, we should try to work 'as if' the way this conversation went is some kind of litmus of the wider issues in the system of work and OD in future. It isn't the truth but it can be a useful rule of thumb, a 'heuristic'. That is to say, for example: "When I walk through the front door of the organisation, *it's as if* the way the receptionist greets me tells me something straight away about the culture here". It is helpful in developing quick hypotheses as you go about experiencing the system you are working with. So if we apply the 'as if' principle to these conversations, it suggests a number of interesting hypotheses that are thrown up by our imaginal working:

- That imagination works in helping people come to grips with challenging issues – it is a validation of the artful approach
- That our imagination isn't about the future, it is about now
- That the possibilities of a post-human future throw up opportunities and challenges in large and equal measure, in the world of work and life generally
- That OD people need to pick up the baton of helping to meet these challenges, as an ethical position
- That strong feelings will be evoked by the challenges of future work, feelings of powerlessness and anxiety as well as excitement, and that the role of OD may be to facilitate the expression and useful engagement with these feelings
- That ethical issues feature and that OD isn't an ethically neutral discipline – that we need to consider the ethics of our practice more centrally as these issues become more figural – the more-than-human workplace will offer us big choices and it is a test of our character to meet these challenges in a more-than-profit-driven way
- That the post human workplace may actually mean a post-management and even a post-organisation workplace, but that if OD isn't called 'OD' anymore, the skills of facilitating relationships and making meaning will still be needed, more than ever, even if in a new guise.

And so it goes on. Our intention for this book was not to write a comfortable textbook on OD, but rather a simultaneously discomforting yet reassuring and encouraging book. This story embodies that. It suggests at one level that the future we face is highly uncertain. But it also suggests that the craft-like and artfully inspired skills that are the inherent core of our practice in OD (and always have been) will always, and perhaps increasingly, be in demand.

Photo: © Steve Marshall, www.drstevemarshall.com, @drstevemarshall

Concluding thoughts

L IFE IS MESSY AND we shouldn't pretend otherwise. Why should OD, the practice of change in human systems, be otherwise? Of course, there are techniques and tools that aim to simplify matters, but our work is essentially emergent, contested and constantly under formation. We are constantly under formation ourselves. This should be a source of inspiration to us, even though sometimes it feels deeply uncomfortable. Patterns of human interaction occur that we call culture and organisational change. If we take this idea seriously, it raises important questions as to how we develop our practice and work ethically with our clients. It challenges what we mean by 'OD' and further still, it undermines the assumptions that we make about what an organisation is and our role in organising. In unravelling these ideas, our aim is to enable the OD practitioner to do something practical: to help examine and explore practice from a more reflexive and relational basis, where attention is paid to interaction and events can be supported and steered as they are happening in the moment.

As we said in Chapter 1, this is a process of joint inquiry with you the reader that engages the full range of knowing – logical argument, emotion, artistry, an appreciation of knack and even cunning. We have been cautious of being overly didactic, accepting that whilst we can share our views, backed up with evidence, other approaches work as well. In short, we have approached writing this book in a way consistent with our OD practice: that of being reflexive, listening to ourselves and others as we make sense of what we do and make progress.

But sometimes, we are pushed by our students or clients to say 'what the answer is'. They don't have the time or patience for us to retort with another question, such as: "Well, it depends. What do you think?!" Their request for some home truths puts us in a paradoxical position, even an ethical dilemma. To withhold may offer them the chance to muddle through of their own accord which, ultimately, is often the best way; but it may also seem uncharitable and even perverse. So how can we answer them in a way that means they don't hold our view as *the* view, and shut down their exploration of other avenues? This is another opportunity for craft.

So, with a warning in place that we are at risk of contradicting everything we have said, here are some thoughts about what might be our 'dos and don'ts' of OD. This isn't 'the answer', of course, but rather an offering of insights. Feel free to take them or leave them. In that spirit, we say:

- There is only one practice, one craft that needs to make sense to you and that is your own, because it sits in a context that is local, timely and specific. Develop your articulation of and confidence about how it works.
- Your relationships are vital, in work and beyond. They are the main stuff of OD. They can be seen as an asset, but be wary of how that objectifies them. Make an ongoing choice about how far you are prepared to use your relationships in this way.
- Organisations and the teams and groups in them are based on assumptions that can be challenged – which as an OD person, is your role. This process starts by challenging your own assumptions.
- As a friend of ours says, "Stick with the question. Answers have a short shelf life."
- Embrace the unintended consequences of your own actions and those of others. Things shouldn't go according to plan.
- Pay attention to those voices not being heard.
- As a 'person of colour' (which we all are), your story and your difference are tools you can choose to use. Indeed, they are perhaps among the most valuable ones you have, so make sure the purpose you are putting them to is one that makes your heart sing.
- OD people can use all sorts of different sources of 'knowledge' and meaning-making. Indeed, being the storyteller and dreamer of dreams might be the vital role you play.
- Develop your artful practice – or perhaps notice what part of your practice is already artful and imaginative, and set about amplifying it. It will give you and others hope, energy and life.
- Connect and do rather than strategise; the best work happens in the moment of contact.
- You are making ethical choices in your work – make these explicit as part of your practice.
- Evaluate your work in human terms. The evidence of its impact is about real people and what matters to you and them.
- Everybody can point to what needs fixing in the system, yet we know that "we don't see the world as it is, but as we are", as the Talmud says. So you may as well focus on developing your own understanding of

yourself as you land in the world of others. We call this reflexivity and it is not about being self-absorbed. Ironically, being more reflexive could be one of the most selfless developmental moves you can make.

So there you go. In full knowledge of the irony of saying this immediately after the above list, we have nevertheless been keen not to offer simplistic solutions or a 'how to' text book. Instead, with the use of practical examples, fiction and some philosophical ideas, we have sought to build bridges between our worlds of OD and yours. The connections that you make are of course up to you and each person's perspective will be different, as indeed are ours as authors. We draw on ideas of craft and art, and the underlying principles as to how knowledge is continuingly developed, with each unique context, paying attention to practical wisdom, knack and cunning.

As we move into a future of deeper machine learning and automation, it might be tempting to lose sight of the power of human-to-human interaction – to see OD as a collection of techniques and algorithms to be applied without continuingly challenging ourselves with those fundamental questions as to what we are doing, why we are doing it and what might be the longer-term impacts on people. We see a continued blind faith in algorithms as a considerable threat to OD and its goals. In the aftermath of the Second World War, the likes of Kurt Lewin aimed to improve the world of work. Although working conditions have changed, they have not always done so for the better. If OD is to have relevance both organisationally and in society, challenging questions as to what we are doing and for what purpose need to be asked *and* acted upon. These questions are difficult and need to be asked of everyone, including our clients and people in power. These conversations require a deeper and more sophisticated ability to understand and interact with the wider systems that we are part of. We are hopeful that OD practitioners will step up to this challenge and begin to have those conversations and engagements in organisations. With a greater reliance on machine learning and big data, we hope that people will have the capacity to ask and address these more fundamental issues. And we have a role in facilitating this.

It is ironic that as we become more expert, we jump to self-affirming solutions and are increasingly less aware of the array of possibilities available to us. This is true not only for our own practice, but also of the people in the organisations that we work with. For much of the time, these shortcuts are helpful in making us more efficient. But not always: opportunities can be missed, and we may miss the opportunity for being reflexive. Whilst expertise is to be welcomed and encouraged, it is important to avoid complacency and an over reliance on existing practice. For us, this raises the importance of diversity, both in terms of culture and in ways of thinking, in order to continuingly ask those challenging questions without which developments in life, in work and in OD cannot occur.

Acting ethically is important, but the way that we think about ethics needs to be challenged. It is not sufficient to think about ethics as an activity to be carried out beforehand, for example in a few lines in an OD proposal. Given what we have already said about the emergent and evolving nature of OD, a different form of ethics is required. This is one whereby we pay attention to the 'micro-ethical dilemmas' as they occur in real time as we engage with people; for example, who do we invite to a conversation and who do we not; what are the implications for people who we might not know, and for the future in those conversations that we have with a CEO on her restructuring plans? These are real-time ethical dilemmas.

Associated with ethics is the issue of risk; any activity or conversation we embark on comes with a hope of some improvement, but this can never be guaranteed and events can take an opposite turn, with unexpected or unknown factors. These can affect not only our client and the wider organisation but also ourselves. What are the conversations that we need to have to explore this honestly? It is not ethical to avoid conversations about possible negative outcomes or to promise positive certainty.

Writing this book has mirrored our own OD practice. We have brought our entire selves to this, to reflexively explore our own craft, and we invite you to do likewise. So when James, for example, talks of his time in the boat yard, the implications this had for his own practice and the metaphors that he draws on, the question is: what are formative experiences and analogies that ring true for you, and why? The use of our imagination, for example introducing Jas and Imogen, has been important for us to challenge our own thinking about the nature of organisations. Not only has this challenged our thinking as individuals, it has also affected the conversations we had between ourselves and with others. What fictional accounts might you draw upon and how might these affect your thinking and conversations? The point we are keen to emphasise is that it is very difficult to see and challenge the assumptions that come to form our daily lives; but the use of imaginative prompts can enable us to see things differently. All of this is to develop better organisations.

According to the ancient expression, it takes a village to raise a child. We are mindful that it is the same for an OD practitioner or for the authors of a book on OD. We are grateful to friends, family, colleagues and clients who have given us the space to play and learn. Our hope for you is that you may be similarly blessed.

Glossary

THIS GLOSSARY IS NOT intended to give definitive descriptions of terms used; instead, it offers offer a quick reference as to how we engaged with the terms.

Assumptions
: Pre-existing attitudes and thoughts one has. These may either be accessible and easy to describe or deep seated and hard to give voice to.

Complexity
: Nonlinear relationship between initial conditions and what might emerge in the future. A way of thinking that moves beyond the more Newtonian assumptions of cause and effect.

Diversity
: Difference, in identities as well as thinking, and how we relate to and work with that difference, both formally and informally.

Narrative
: A first-person account of an event that at the time of the occurrence *or* of writing has come to influence how an individual understands their practice and thought.

Organisation development
: The processes of deliberate and emergent change in the structures, cultures and practices of human systems.

P(p)olitics
: The informal and formal enacting of change and the impact this has on others. Related to power.

Power
: The ability both formally and informally to make or prevent change in human and technological systems. It is a ubiquitous feature of human relating whereby one person has influence over another.

Reflexivity	A complex set of ideas suggesting a state or a discipline of self-awareness or of questioning what one has said or done. Here we stress the practice of thinking critically about one's practice, which will affect one's future practice.
Risk	The capacity of acts or events to change in unknown ways the power and identity relationships between people (as well as material resources).
Systems	Interconnected and interrelated dynamic of human and more-than-human interactions that undergo processes of change and evolution over time. These are something that we are part of with no option of 'stepping into' or 'stepping out from'.

References

Alvesson, M., and Skoldberg, K. (2009) *Reflexive Methodology – New Vistas for Qualitative Research*, second edition, Sage, London.

Alvesson, M., and Spicer, A. (2012) 'A Stupidity-Based Theory of Organizations', *Journal of Management Studies*, Vol. 49, No. 7, pp.1,194–220.

Arendt, H. (1963) *Eichmann in Jerusalem*, Penguin, London.

Bateson, G. (1972) *Steps to an Ecology of Mind*, University of Chicago Press, Chicago.

Baumard, P. (1999) *Tacit Knowledge in Organizations*, Sage, London.

Bevan, H. (2011) *Part 2 – Leading Large Scale Change: The Postscript*, NHS Institute for Innovation and Improvement.

Bevan, H., Plesk, P., and Winstanley, L. (2011) 'Part 1 – a practical guide', *Leading Large Scale Change*, NHS Institute for Innovation and Improvement.

Block, P. (2011) *Flawless Consulting: A Guide to Getting Your Expertise Used*, Pfeiffer.

Bortoft, H. (1998) 'Counterfeit and authentic wholes: finding a means of dwelling on nature', in Seamon, D., and Kajonc, A., (eds), *Goethe's Way of Science – A Phenomenology of Nature*, State University of New York, New York, pp.277–99.

Bourdieu, P. (1998) 'Is a Disinterested Act Possible?', in Bourdieu, P., (ed.), *Practical Reason: On the Theory of Action*, Polity Press, Cambridge, UK.

Burnes, B. (2004) 'Kurt Lewin and the Planned Approach to Change: A Re-appraisel', *Journal of Management Studies*, Vol. 41, No. 6, pp.977–1,002.

Cheung-Judge, M., and Holbeche, L. (2015) *Organization Development: A Practitioner's Guide for OD and HR*, second edition, Kogan Page Publishers, London and Philadelphia.

Chippindale, C. (2000) 'Capta and Data: On the True Nature of Archaeological Information', *American Antiquity*, Vol. 65, No. 4, pp.605–12.

Clarkson, P. (1993) 'Bystander games', *Transactional Analysis Journal*, Vol. 23, No. 3, pp.158–72.

Collins, J. (2001) *Good to Great*, Random House.

Connell, R. (2005) *Masculinities*, second eddition, Polity Press, Cambridge.

Cunliffe, A. (2009) 'The Philosopher Leader: On Relationalism, Ethics and Reflexivity – A Critical Perspective to Teaching Leadership', *Management Learning*, Vol. 40, No. 1, pp.87–101.

Dawkins, R. (1996) *The Blind Watchmaker: Why the Evidence of Evolution Reveals a Universe without Design*, Penguin, London.

DeCerteau, M. (1984) *The Practice of Everyday Life*, University of California Press, Berkeley.

Detienne, M., and Vernant, J. (1991) *Cunning Intelligence in Greek Culture and Society*, edited by Lloyd, J., University of Chicago Press, Chicago.

Dewey, J. (2007) *Democracy and Education*, Echo Library, Teddington.

Economist (2017) 'Carry on doctor: Britain's doctors revolt against plans for a seven-day service', *Economist*, London, pp.20–2.

Ellis, C., and Bochner, A.P. (1996) *Composing Ethnography – Alternative Forms of Qualitative Writing*, AltaMira, Walnut Creek, London and New York.

Finney, L., and Jefkins, C. (2009) 'Best Practice in OD Evaluation – Understanding the impact of organisational development', Roffey Park, Horsham.

Francis, H., Holbeche, L., and Reddington, M. (2012) *People and Organisational Development: A New Agenda for Organisational Effectiveness*, CIPD, London.

Franck, F. (1973) *The Zen of Seeing: Seeing/Drawing as Meditation*, Vintage, New York.

Freire, P. (1996) *Pedagogy of the Oppressed*, new revised edition, Penguin, London.

Gallie, W. (1956) 'Essentially Contested Concepts', *Proceedings of the Aristotelian Society*, Vol. 56, pp.167–98.

Gardner, D. (2012) *Future Babble: How to Stop Worrying and Love the Unpredictable*, Random House, London.

Gergen, K., and Gergen, M. (2008) 'Social Construction and Reserach as Action', *The SAGE Handbook of Action Research: Participative Inquiry: Participative Inquiry and Practice*, second edition, Sage, London, pp.159–71.

Goldacre, B. (2008) *Bad Science*, HarperCollins, New York.

Grey, C. (2009) *A Very Short, Fairly Interesting and Reasonably Cheep Book About Studying Organiazions*, Sage.

Grosz, E.A. (2004) *The Nick of Time: Politics, Evolution, and the Untimely*, Duke University Press.

Hancock, P. (2008) 'Embodied Generosity and Ethics of Organisation', *Organization Studies*, Vol. 29, No. 10, pp.1,357–73.

Hernes, T. (2014) 'Alfred North Whitehead', in Helin, J., Hernes, T., and Holt, R. (eds), *The Oxford Handbook of Process Philosophy & Organization Studies* (pp.255–72), Oxford: Oxford University Press.

Heron, J. (1992) *Feeling and Personhood: Psychology in Another Key*, Sage Publications, London.

Heron, J., and Reason, P. (2008) 'Extending epistemology within a co-operative inquiry', in Reason, P., and Bradbury, H., (eds), *Handbook of Action Research*, second edition, Sage Publications, London, pp.366–80.

Herzberg, F. (1968) 'One more time: How do you motivate employees?', *Harvard Business Review*, Vol. 46, pp.53–62.

Ho, K. (2009) *Liquidated: An Ethnography of Wall Street*, Durham and London.

Hochschild, A. (2003) *The Managed Heart: Commercialization of Human Feeling*, second edition, University of California Press, Oakland.

Holbeche, L. (2012) 'Organisational effectiveness: A fresh mindset', *People Management*, February, pp.32–7.

Jameson, F. (2005) *Archaeologies of the Future: The Desire Called Utopia and Other Science Fictions*, Verso, London and New York.

Kemmis, S. (2001) 'Exploring the relevance of critical theory for action research: Emancipatory action research in the footsteps of Jurgen Habermas', in Reason, P., and Bradbury, H., (eds), *Handbook of Action Research: Participative Inquiry and Practice*, SAGE, p.468.

Kessel, M. (2011) 'The problems with today's pharmaceutical business – an outsider's view', *Nature Biotechnology*, Vol. 29, No. 1, p.27.

Kotter, J. (1996) *Leading Change*, Harvard Business Press.

Lewis, L. (2017) 'Unspoken word behind a string of Japanese scandals', *Financial Times*, London, 31 March, available at: https://www.ft.com/content/c34706d6-13da-11e7-b0c1-37e417ee6c76?accessToken=zwAAAVsj2WcwkdPDRwbWE9oR59OwwTfkF-5sdg.MEYCIQCQBejM9eogFOsojyEUv6UvCOcnTh1_Aj2NfBMbvGsd3AlhAM6BVXisotPVri_htPFAQbLLSvpqCmbDRCCYta6gQO6-&sharetype=gift#comments.

Malhotra, R. (2016) 'Ants trapped in nuclear bunker are developing their own society', *New Scientist*, available at: https://www.newscientist.com/article/mg23130904-400-ants-trapped-in-nuclear-bunker-are-developing-their-own-society/ (accessed 23 July 2017).

Mead, G.H. (1932) *The Philosophy of the Present*, Prometheus Books, Amherst, New York.

Mead, G.H. (1934) *Mind, Self and Society*, Chicago University, Chicago.

Mintzberg, H., Ahlstrand, A., and Lampel, J. (2005) *Strategy Bites Back: It Is a Lot More, and Less, than You Ever Imagined*, Pearson Education, London.

Morgan, G. (2006) *Images of Organization*, Sage, London.

Neurath, O. (1944) 'Sociology and the Practice of Life', *International Encyclopedia of Unified Science*, Vol. 2, No. 1, pp.42–7.

Oshry, B. (1995) *Seeing Systems: Unlocking the Mysteries of Organizational Life*, Berrett-Koehler, San Francisco.

Pedler, M. (2011) *Action Learning in Practice*, Gower Publishing Ltd, Farnham.

Peters, T. (1991) 'Chaos Theory's Premature Promise', available at: http://tompeters.com/columns/chaos-theorys-premature-promise/ (accessed 29 August 2017).

Pollner, M. (1991) 'Left of Ethnomethodology: The Rise and Decline of Radical Reflexivity', *American Sociological Review*, Vol. 56, No. 3, pp.370–80.

Raymer, D., Schroeder, D., Blankenship, D., Young, D., Quartini, E., and Sheet, A. (2014) 'Social Sciences-Psychological and Cognitive Sciences: Adam DI Kramer, Jamie E. Guillory, and Jeffrey T. Hancock, Experimental evidence of massive-scale emotional contagion through social networks', *Proceedings of the National Academy of Sciences*, Vol. 111, No. 24, pp.8,788–90.

Revans, R. (1998) *ABC of Action Learning: Empowering Managers to Act and to Learn*, Lemos and Crane.

Schön, D. (1991) *The Reflective Practitioner – How Professionals Think in Action*, Ashgate, Aldershot.

Scott, J.C. (1990) *Domination and the Arts of Resistance – Hidden Transcripts*, Yale University Press, New Haven and London.

Scott, J.C. (1998) *Seeing Like a State: How Certain Schemes to Improve the Human Condition Have Failed*, Yale University Press.

Seamon, D. (1998) 'Goethe, Nature and Phenomenology – An introduction', *Goethe's Way of Science – A Phenomenology of Nature*, State University of New York, New York.

Seeley, C., and Thornhill, E. (2014) *Artful Organisation*, Ashridge Business School, Berkhamsted.

Sennett, R. (2008) *The Craftsman*, Penguin, London.

Serres, M. (1991) *The Troubadour of Knowledge*, University of Michigan Press.

Shaw, P. (2002) *Changing Conversations in Organizations – A Complexity Approach to Change*, Routledge, Abingdon, UK.

Shotter, J. (2005) 'Understanding Process From Within: An Argument for "Withness"-Thinking', *Organization Studies*, Vol. 27, No. 4, pp.585–604.

Slezkine, Y. (2004) *The Jewish Century*, Princeton University Press, Princeton, New Jersey.

Smith, W., Higgins, M., and Parker, M., (eds) (2001) 'Introduction, More Amazing Tales', *Science Fiction and Organziation*, Routledge, London, pp.1–11.

Stacey, R. (2001) *Complex Responsive Processes in Organizations – Learning and Knowledge Creation*, Routledge, London and New York.

Stacey, R. (2006) 'Learning as an Activity of Interdependent People', in MacIntosh, R., MacLean, D., Stacey, R., and Griffin, D., (eds), *Complexity and Organisation – Readings and Conversations*, Routledge, London, pp.237–46.

Steier, F. (1991) 'Introduction – Research as Self Reflexivity, Self Reflexivity as Social Process', in Steier, F., (ed.), *Research and Reflexivity – Inquiries in Social Construction*, Sage Publications, London, pp.1–11.

Steyaert, C. (2014) 'Michel Serres', in Helin, J., Hernes, T., Hjorth, D., and Holt, R., (eds), *The Oxford Handbook of Process Philosophy & Organization Studies*, Oxford University Press, Oxford, pp.549–84.

Tucker, A. (1998) *Anthony Giddens and Modern Social Theory*, Sage Publications, London.

Wachowski, L., and Wachowski, L. (1999) *The Matrix*, US.

Warwick, R. (2016) 'Doubt, uncertainty and vulnerability in leadership: using fiction to enable reflection and voice', *Tamara: Journal for Critical Organization Inquiry*, Vol. 14, No. 4, pp.127–37.

Warwick, R., and Board, D. (2013) *The Social Development of Leadership and Knowledge: A Reflexive Inquiry Into Research and Practice*, Palgrave Macmillan., Basingstoke.

Warwick, R., McCray, J., and Board, D. (2017) 'Bourdieu's habitus and field: implications on the practice and theory of critical action learning', *Action Learning: Research and Practice*, Taylor & Francis, Vol. 14, No. 2, pp.104–19.

Warwick, R., McCray, J., and Palmer, A. (2017) 'Action learning: ripples within and beyond the set', *Leadership in Health Services*, Vol. 30, No. 2.

Weick, K.E. (1995) *Sensemaking in Organizations*, Sage, London.

Weisbord, M.R. (2004) *Productive Workplaces Revisited: Dignity, Meaning, and Community in the 21st Century*, Jossey-Bass, San Francisco.

Wheatley, M. (1999) *Leadership and the New Science – Discovering Order in a Chaotic World*, Berrett-Koehler Publishers, San Fransisco.

Wittgenstein, L. (1969) *On Certainty*, edited by Anscombe, G., and von Wright, G., Harper Torchbooks, New York.

Wright Mills, C. (1959) *The Sociological Imagination*, Oxford University Press, Oxford.

Contents Index

Author Index